"Davis thematically organizes stories of noteworthy figures in twelve chapters featuring titles such as "I Am Beautiful" and "I Believe in Myself..." The result is a narrative that's both serious and upbeat, suited for children to read independently as well as for parents to read aloud...An attractively illustrated, engaging book that skillfully balances pride in the past with awareness of 21st-century challenges."
— Kirkus Review

"... beautiful and important book that delighted my heart in a way very few books have. As an educator... I would like to see this book as compulsory reading in schools where mostly African American students are served. I have never seen such a positive, empowering resource to celebrate brown skin and encourage young people to overcome challenges and be proud of where they come from and the skin they are in. A fabulous book..." — Kelley Rhoads, Educator

"Uplifting. Smart. Hopeful. This book reminds and expands our thinking on race today. I am so glad it is for grades 4 and up. I will order this book for our library. — Linda George, Librarian

"When Julia Davis's grandson asked her if her brown skin made her sad, Davis was inspired to write a book about her pride in her brown-skinned forebears...Davis goes all the way back to Africa...slavery...and...the Civil Rights Movement...I love her positive attitude...I Like My Brown Skin Because...will inspire young readers (old ones, too!) and instill an appreciation for...Black people throughout American history. It's a hall of heroes; pick your role model... It's a great book! Buy it for your kids." — Paul Mastin, Reviewer, Independent Book Publishers Association

"Well-written, easy to read, full of valuable information. The Precious Children sections are so personalized that children think their own grandmothers are talking to them. I can't wait to read it to my students." — Mikasa Simms, Educator

"I love this book. It gives children hope. Julia Davis has translated the difficult subject of "race" into clear and concise language. By letting children know that we all have choices about how we treat each other, I Like My Brown Skin Because... helps usher in a future that allows people of all colors to be treated with dignity and respect." — Lauren Heaton, Reporter, The Yellow Springs News

"At first I thought I Like My Brown Skin Because... was only for African American children. I was wrong. After reading it, I googled 'children and racism' and found a blog on parenting.com by a white woman who was mortified when she asked her small daughter why she did not like a nanny applicant. The child answered with a question, 'Because I don't like her brown skin?' This book is equally for European Americans — most of whom do not want their children to live with the terrible limitations of prejudice." — Barbara Kneipp, Marketing Manager

# I Like My Brown Skin Because...

## Celebrating the Heritage *of* African American Children

*by* JULIA A. DAVIS

Epps-Alford Publishing
Yellow Springs, Ohio

# I Like My Brown Skin Because...
## Celebrating The Heritage *of* African American Children

Epps-Alford Publishing
P. O. Box 504
Yellow Springs, Ohio 45387
(937) 215-3818
www.epps-alford.com
email: info@epps-alford.com

# Table of Contents

## About The Author

Julia A. Davis holds a Bachelor's Degree in history from Earlham College, a Master's Degree in history from the University of Dayton, and a Master of Arts in Conflict Resolution from Antioch University. She has taught world history and American history at the middle school level, the high school level, and the college level. She enjoys writing and she enjoys traveling to places she has taught about in her history classes. She is a member of St. John Missionary Baptist Church, and a member of Delta Sigma Theta Sorority Inc.

## Acknowledgments

I cannot imagine writing a book of this magnitude without input from a variety of people whose willingness to read and make suggestions would help make this presentation very special for young people. Many thanks to Mikasa Simms, John Gudgel, Judy Skillings, Linda Smith, John Sidney, Patricia Coleman, Genevie Foy, Roslyn Bacon, Nacim McIlhargey Sabaja, Sherry Robinson, Jeff Craig, Jennifer Davis, Lauren Heaton, Shirley Smith, Annette McGee Wright, Ethel Washington-Harris, Teri Smalls, Laura Lewis, David Miller, Julia White, Kevin McGruder, Anthony Alford, and Chet and Kyra Robinson. They took time from their busy schedules to read what I had written, and then they made comments that encouraged me and helped me.

My general editor is also my best friend, Julia Frazier White. She has been my sounding board for every book I have ever written.

I thank the artists who contributed to this book. Abner Cope is a retired associate professor of art at Central State University (Ohio). Alpha Frierson and Emmanuel Mooty are two of his former students. Much gratitude to Deb Slater for her cover design and her page layout.

*To My Husband, Who Encouraged Me.*

*For John Christian And All Children Whose Questions Must Be Answered*

*"The arc of the moral universe is long but it bends toward justice."*

Dr. Martin Luther King, Jr.

# Prologue

## Answering The Questions Of A Child

*I Like My Brown Skin Because...* was written after a four-year-old asked his grandmother if her brown skin ever made her sad, and then asked her why she liked her brown skin so much. "I was shocked by his words and I knew my grandchild was hurting."

This must-read book is an answer to his question. The author begins by saying all skin is good, and it is healthy for you to like the skin you are in. Then she highlights her special reasons for liking her brown skin. Throughout her narrative she shares personal experiences and gives sound advice that is full of wisdom.

*I Like My Brown Skin Because...* is a conversation launch pad for parents and children of every background – black, white, yellow, brown, red and mixed. It is for all families who want their children to live in a way that honors all people. It is for all people who want to understand the history behind the "racial" tension in the United States today.

The constant refrain of this book is, "I like my brown skin: I like me." People of all colors who feel good about themselves like other people regardless of skin color. They have enough love in their hearts to treat everybody with respect and dignity. *I Like My Brown Skin Because...*allows children to see that all people have choices: we can do what is right or we can do what is wrong. In every situation, each one of us has a choice.

The 156 pages of text and illustrations in *I Like My Brown Skin Because...* are divided into twelve chapters that introduce children to the African American story. With plenty of illustrations, even the child who is not reading will soon be "reading" the messages on each page. Older children will go to the library to get more detailed accounts of what they have read in *I Like My Brown Skin Because…*

*I Like My Brown Skin Because…* is told sensitively, intelligently, and lovingly. The love and hope of a grandmother shine through this book. It is appropriate for people of all ages, and it is concise and easy to read. It highlights the fact that the United States is best when all people are valued. *I Like My Brown Skin Because…* gives children an opportunity to see that positive actions taken by people of every color have moved the United States closer to becoming "…one nation under God with liberty and justice for all."

## A Note To Parents And Teachers: What Are Our Children Thinking?
### (*Please read.*)

African American children today are living in a nation that preaches equal opportunity for all, while practicing a policy of white privilege and black suppression. In every aspect of American life, children are programmed to see white people as the norm and to see black people as less than this norm. All around us are negative messages about African Americans. Rarely do newspapers, magazines, radio programs, and television programs present the millions of African Americans who go to work everyday and make great contributions to themselves and to this country. Very seldom do the media outlets discuss white privilege and racial profiling that assume innocence on the part of Europeans and guilt on the part of African Americans. Nor do we hear about "white privilege" that propels European Americans to the top regardless of their background and qualifications.

Whether in the poor house or the White House, African Americans are treated as outsiders. They are appreciated when the majority society wants someone to entertain, play basketball, clean, cook, take care of children, or do hard and dangerous work. They are under-appreciated when they are equipped with stellar qualifications and have positions of leadership.

None of this is lost on our children. Since birth, they have spent most of their time observing. As a result, children recognize the elephant in the room that adults know is there but do not talk about. That elephant is racism: it is the fact that in American society, positions of power have traditionally been reserved for European Americans and positions of servitude are reserved for African Americans. Children see this at the grocery store, at the shopping mall, at the bank, at the post office, at amusement parks, in newspapers and magazines, on billboards, and on television. They even see it on U.S. money (paper currency and coins).

In segregated neighborhoods they see limited options. In desegregated neighborhoods, they are often among so few black people that they are prone to think about African Americans, and even the color black, in the same way that their white schoolmates think. As a result, we hear them make self-negating statements that shock us.

I have noticed these statements and conclusions among my own children, even as my husband and I worked tirelessly to give them a deep understanding of African American history and exposed them to outstanding African American role models. Unfortunately, this exposure did not seem to shield my children from moments of negative self-identification.

I recall my first-born at four years old watching a telephone repairman as he restored a phone line outside our house. I was shocked when my child declared, "When I grow up, I will turn white and be a telephone man, too."

My second-born made similar statements. One day we were driving behind a car moving much slower than the minimum highway speed limit. When my husband started to pass the car, our son said, "Stop, Daddy, don't do that. You'll get in trouble for passing a white person."

Over the years, I have heard these statements from African American children in my neighborhood, at my church, and in my high school classes. I recall a good friend's son who was the only African American in his middle school. In one year, three pairs of sticks for his snare drum, two pairs of gym shoes, and one calculator were stolen from his locker. He never verbally assigned a color to the face of the person(s) who stole them. One day when he and his mother were driving through a neighborhood that is predominantly African American, he said, "Let's lock the doors. These people steal."

I am reminded of my young friend Karen, a chemistry professor at a local university, who dropped her daughter off at a highly ranked daycare center every day. One cold morning as she kissed Sarah "Good-bye," Karen said, "Sweet Heart, I miss you everyday. One of these days I'm going to stay here and be your teacher." Her daughter's response was, "Mommy, you can't do that. You have to be white to be the teacher."

With video recordings of police officers killing unarmed African American males in the past few years, many Children of Color are afraid. Some have nightmares about these killings and others verbalize their fears when awake. A colleague was driving her 11-year-old son to the library when she noticed him slumped over in the back seat of the car. He had slumped down when he saw a police car on the side of the road. "If the police don't see me," the child said, "they won't shoot me."

While African American children are feeling left out and inadequate, most European American children are feeling privileged because of their white skin. A European American friend recently told me she was aware of white privilege as early as the first grade when she watched it work to her advantage. Several white boys had been disrupting the class by passing gas, and they all sat on the far side of the room. Rebecca was at a table with two other white girls, two white boys, and an African American boy named Charles. One day Rebecca passed gas and the noise caused the class to laugh. The teacher looked at her table and said, "Who did that?" Rebecca knew that if she just sat quietly, Mrs. Schultz would blame Charles. A few seconds later, Mrs. Schultz said, "Charles, go to the office." Ashamed that she let Charles get blamed for what she did, Rebecca did not tell this story until she was in college.

Perhaps the saddest experience for me, and the one that prompted me to write this book, occurred a few months ago. It was a bright November morning when my 4½-year-old grandson, John Christian, and I left a going-out-of-business sale at a major discount store. I had purchased shirts for the pre-school youngster, and a book that would help him with sounds and word parts for reading. When I told him he could select one toy that costs less than $10, he chose a dinosaur with a plastic skeleton and rubber skin that could be removed to show the skeleton. This child was really into dinosaurs and he was happy to have his new Para-sau-rol-ophus. With much excitement, he told me what dinosaurs ate, and how they became extinct. As we were leaving the store, he showed me how dinosaurs walked.

On the way home, John Christian was securely locked in his car seat, taking off the skin of the dinosaur and putting it back on. I was thinking about making soup and sandwiches for lunch. I looked into the rearview mirror and saw him holding the dinosaur. Our eyes met and I smiled at him. Suddenly, as if out of nowhere, he said, "Gram, does your brown skin ever make you sad? Why are we brown? Why do you like your brown skin so much?" His words upset me greatly, and I knew he needed fortification for the world in which we live.

I am a product of the 1960's Civil Rights Movement. I have books and pictures of famous African Americans all over our house, and similar books and pictures are at his house. I had no idea these thoughts were in his mind.

"My Precious Child," I said, "I love my brown skin, and I love your brown skin. Granddaddy loves his brown skin and Mommy loves her brown skin. Your uncles, aunts, and cousins love their brown skin. We will talk more about this when we get home. Traffic is heavy right now and I need to concentrate on driving. Let's listen to your Christmas music while we drive. I love you and I love your brown skin."

While John Christian was taking his afternoon nap, I started jotting down reasons for liking my brown skin. I decided to put these reasons into a story for him, his cousins, and their friends of all colors. *I Like My Brown Skin Because…* is the text of my story.

## A Note To John Christian And All Children

My beautiful, brown skin always makes me happy. It has never made me sad. But I do feel sad when I meet people who treat others in a mean way because of their skin color. I feel sad for the person who is being mean and I feel sad for the person who is being mistreated. Some people do not have enough love in their hearts to treat all people with love. Often they feel unloved themselves and they are hurting so much inside that they hurt others. Occasionally you will run into people in this condition. Just remember who you are, remember that you are loved, and remember all the good things you can do with your life. Also remember that there are plenty of people who judge a person on character rather than on color. The election of President Barack Obama is proof of that.

I am writing this story to tell you why I like my brown skin. But first, I want you to know that skin is merely an outside covering for the wonderful person you are inside your skin. It is good and healthy for each person in the world to like his or her skin, and to like every physical characteristic he or she has. If my skin were blue, I would be telling you why I like that color. Liking your skin is a part of liking yourself. I like my skin: I like me. When you like yourself, you can also like people who have skin that is different from yours.

I like my family's brown skin because it is beautiful and strong. Some of us are a rich, dark, delicious chocolate brown. Others are medium brown, light brown, yellow-brown, red-brown, and olive-brown. Many people who are not considered brown admire our skin colors. They flock to the beach, go to tanning booths, and lie in the sun to become the colors we are. They do this even at the risk of developing skin cancer.

Anthropologists and other scientists say that the first people on earth were dark-skinned people who lived in Africa. All people on earth are descendants of these dark-skinned people.

Scientists also tell us about a substance in each person's skin called melanin. The darker a person is, the more melanin he has in his skin. Our skin is brown because of the amount of melanin in it. Nature is full of diversity and differences. All people on earth are different colors, different sizes, and different shapes. People also have different mental abilities, different physical abilities, different talents, and different personalities.

When I see my beautiful brown face in the mirror, I see brown people who did great things before me, brown people who are doing great things now, and brown people who will still be doing great things when I am no longer here.

I will say it again: I love my brown skin. I like the pride that comes from my heritage. I am from a people of winners, a people who cannot be defeated. I am from a brilliant people who excel in every endeavor. You will understand my pride as you read *I Like My Brown Skin Because...*

In the United States today there are more than three hundred million (300,000,000) people. All of them have ancestors who were immigrants to this country. Some came here from Africa, some from Europe, and some from Asia.

Persons who originated in the same part of the world had similar color in their skin. The people from Africa had black or brown skin and very curly hair. Most people from Europe had light skin and very straight hair. Some people from Asia had a yellow tint to their skin. Others had brown skin with a reddish tint. All human beings look alike under the skin.

Regardless of skin color, each and every person in this world has been "created equal." And in the words of the Declaration of Independence, they have been "...endowed by their Creator with certain unalienable Rights, that among these are Life, Liberty, and the pursuit of Happiness."

Many people in the United States today are a mixture of Europeans, Africans, and Asians. Together, Americans are a beautiful montage of colors and physical characteristics. Most African Americans were brought here from West Africa. This book introduces you to their history. African American history makes me very proud of my brown skin and my African features.

• • •

# Old African Kingdoms

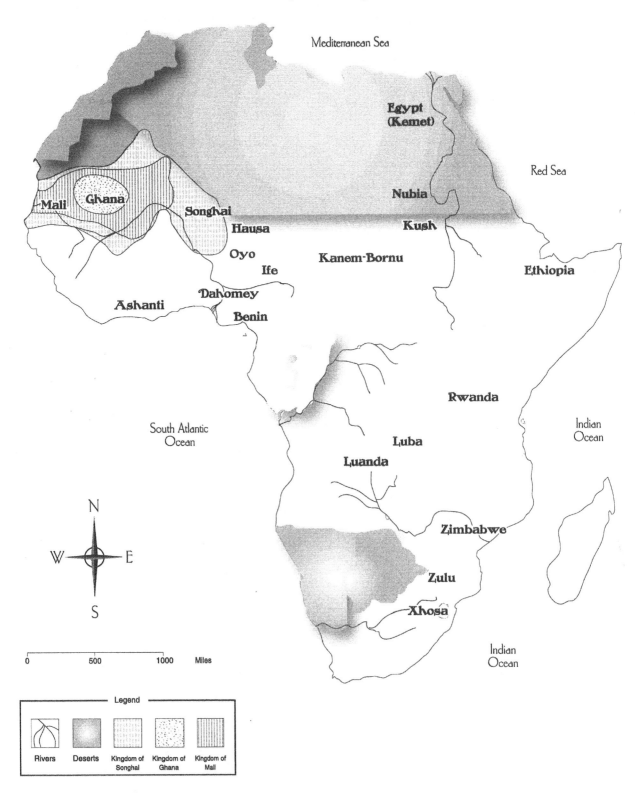

Mediterranean Sea

Egypt
(Kemet)

Red Sea

Mali

Ghana

Songhai

Nubia

Hausa

Kush

Oyo

Ife

Kanem-Bornu

Ethiopia

Ashanti

Dahomey

Benin

Rwanda

South Atlantic
Ocean

Luba

Luanda

Indian
Ocean

Zimbabwe

Zulu

N

W E

S

Xhosa

Indian
Ocean

| 0 | 500 | 1000 | Miles |

### Legend

| Rivers | Deserts | Kingdom of Songhai | Kingdom of Ghana | Kingdom of Mali |

# I Like My Brown Skin Because...

## It Reminds Me Of Beautiful African Families.

# I Am Beautiful.

I like my brown skin because beautiful African families make me very proud and very happy to be brown like them. Let me tell you the story of these beautiful African families.

Before they were brought to North America to build the United States, African people had created outstanding civilizations on the huge, mineral-rich continent where they lived. Egypt and Ethiopia, two of the oldest nations in the world, are located in Africa. The great Zulu kingdom and the nation of Great Zimbabwe were located in Africa. These nations were built by People of Color.

**Ghana**, **Mali**, and **Songhay** were three outstanding West African kingdoms. From the 4th century through the 16th century, they were some of the most advanced kingdoms in the world. These kingdoms had highway systems with places for people to rest while on their journeys. They had well-constructed buildings, an organized code of laws, and an advanced knowledge of agriculture and medicine. **Jenne** (jen-neh), **Gao**, and **Timbuktu** were centers of learning in West Africa. Students from all over the Mediterranean world studied at those centers. **Sundiata Keita** and **Mansa Musa** were two of the most outstanding rulers in West Africa. When Mansa Musa ruled Mali, he was worth $400 billion. This makes him the richest man of all times. He made his money through the gold-salt trade. My great ancestors were brought to America from West Africa.

**African families were very strong.** The family was the most important institution in West African societies. Each family member was loved and valued. Family members were counted as wealth and big families that had a lot of people (parents, children, cousins, aunts, uncles, grandparents, etc.) were considered very wealthy.

**West African men** were responsible for seeing that their families were housed, fed, educated, kept safe, and able to enjoy life. Most men were farmers. Others were government officials and judges. Some were medical doctors who helped heal broken bones, and performed cataract surgery on the eyes of elderly people. Still others were merchants, fishermen, salt miners, gold miners, and ironworkers. Men who lived in ancient Ghana were among the first people in the world to smelt iron.

**West African women** who were wives and mothers were busy taking care of their children. In addition, they did the cooking, sewing, washing and housekeeping for their families. Although men prepared the ground, women planted and harvested some of the crops. They were also responsible for drying and storing vegetables, fruits, seafood, fish, and meat. At the marketplace, some women were merchants who sold products made by their husbands.

West African people created good lives for themselves. My brown skin reminds me that I can create a good life for myself, too.

**West African people enjoyed good health.** They ate whole grains, fish and seafood, and plenty of vegetables and fruit. Physical exercise kept them nimble and rarely overweight. European historians

West African people created good lives for themselves. My brown skin reminds me that I can create a good life for myself, too.

commented on the fact that these People of Color had good posture, they had strong, beautiful teeth, and they were very clean people. They were some of the first people in the world to take a bath every day. My brown skin reminds me that I am a descendant of these healthy people: I can eat food that is good for me, I can exercise, and I can be healthy, too.

People in West Africa had a beautiful tradition for introducing a new baby to the village. When a baby was born, the father spent eight days thinking of a name for the infant. On the eighth day he whispered that name into the baby's ear. Then the father held his baby up to the heavens and said, **"Behold, the only One greater than you are."** He wanted the baby to know that no one on earth was inherently superior to his child. After this ceremony, the father introduced his child to the village.

**African children spent most of their time learning.** Their parents carried on intelligent conversations with them and taught them to express themselves with words. Parents taught children to hold their heads up, speak up, and look people in the eyes. They also taught their children good manners. The words *thank you, please,* and *excuse me* will help you throughout life, everywhere you go.

In addition, parents taught their children skills that would prepare them for the world of work. When they became adults, most children did the same work their parents did. Wise elders in the village told children stories that sharpened their ability to think from different points of view. For instance, if the giant wrote *Jack and the Beanstalk*, how would he tell that story differently from how Jack told it? What about the wolf in *The Three Little Pigs*? Would he have given a different ending to that story?

Elders, called *griots* by some African people, taught children history, and parents taught them math. One of the oldest abacus boards in

"Behold, the only One greater than you are."

the world is from West Central Africa. African children enjoyed math games and they enjoyed solving math problems.

When daily chores and educational lessons from parents and elders were over, West African children enjoyed games. Relay races were popular with the boys, and they were very fast runners. (In 2015, Africans were still winning marathons in New York and Boston; and Usain Bolt, a descendant of West Africans, was the fastest man in the world.) Boys also enjoyed ball games, darts, ring tossing, and marbles. Wrestling was a sport that participants *and* spectators liked. Water sports were a source of fun, and a way of getting a temporary break from the sun's unrelenting heat.

Most of the girls engaged in conversations with friends. They also played board games, made interesting collages, and made jewelry. Younger girls made dolls. Boys and girls of all ages enjoyed counting songs and rhyming games, jokes, and riddles.

African children using abacus boards to solve math problems

African artwork

West African people enjoyed **music and art**. They sculpted in wood, stone, clay (terra cotta), and bronze. They were among the first people in the world to produce life-like busts and statues of men and women.

Group singing provided a time of fellowship for African communities. Singers blended their voices in wonderful harmony as they enjoyed rounds and medleys. They also had call-and-response music with one person singing the lead message and the group responding with the chorus. Their musical instruments included **horns, harps, drums, xylophones, and strings**.

Africans also danced. Children enjoyed sitting on the ground watching the dancers twisting and leaping in elaborate costumes. Their agile bodies were extremely well disciplined.

● ● ●

Sundiata Keita was the king who pulled West African civilizations together. He created the brilliant kingdom of Mali.

# Precious Children,

Brown skin is a reminder of beautiful African families, great African civilizations, outstanding African education, and wonderful African art, music, and dance. When you think about brown skin, think about the African ancestors. Are your math skills as good as theirs? Do you imitate their good manners as you say, *please, thank you*, and *excuse me*? Do you hold your head up and speak clearly? Do you look people in the eyes? Are you a critical thinker who looks at situations from every point of view? Do you consider the consequences of everything you do? I like my brown skin because it reminds me of my African ancestors. I like my brown skin: I like me.

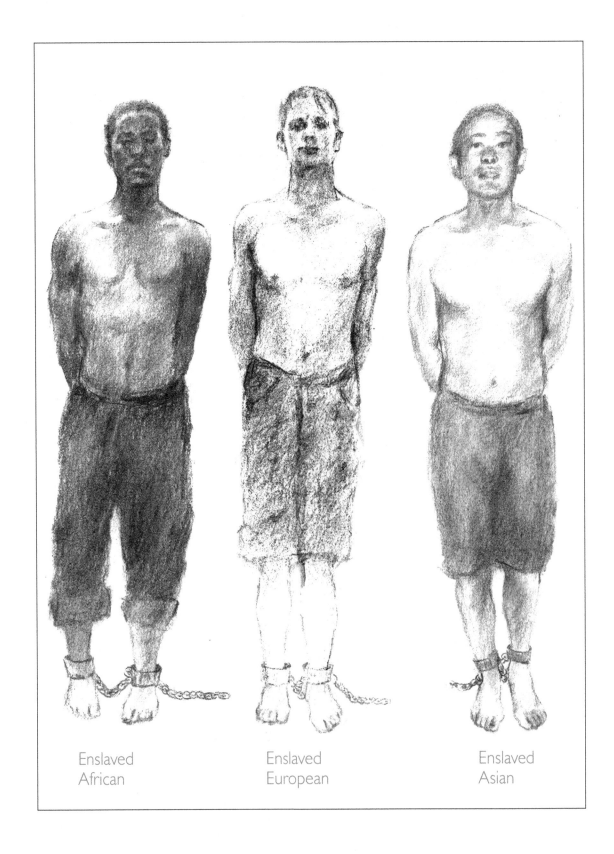

Enslaved
African

Enslaved
European

Enslaved
Asian

## CHAPTER 2

# I Like My Brown Skin Because...

## It Reminds Me That My Ancestors Survived The Evils Of Slavery.

# I Am A Survivor.

Before I say more about why I like my brown skin so much, I must tell you about slavery. Your parents go to work everyday and they are paid money for the work they do. Your parents use the money they make to pay for the house you live in, the heat that keeps you warm, the food you eat, the clothes you wear, and everything else you need.

Getting paid for work you do is a part of today's American economic system. One person agrees to work and one person agrees to pay.

Slavery is not like that. Slavery forces a person to work without pay. Throughout history, people all over the globe have enslaved other people. People of all groups and colors (white, red, black, yellow, and brown) have been forced to work for others without pay. For example, slavery existed in Egypt, classical Greece, and in the Roman Empire. In Medieval Europe, enslaved people were called serfs. They were bought and sold with the land, like houses, trees, and rocks. In China and Japan, when one dynasty (ruling family) conquered another dynasty, many of the defeated people were enslaved.

As Europeans were taking over the New World, they brought Africans to America and forced them to do the work that would

Africans were packed so tightly that many of them died on the trip to America.

develop this country and make many European American families wealthy. Through the **European Trans-Atlantic Slave Trade**, African men, women, and teenagers were captured from their villages. Then they were chained, beaten, and locked in the bottom of a ship for six weeks while the vessel made its way to the Americas. Imagine being in the bottom of a ship that is rocking and reeling, chained to another person so closely that no matter how uncomfortable you are and how much your neck, your back, and your knees may hurt, you cannot get up, or even turn over. Breathing was difficult and many of the kidnapped people died during the journey.

The European Trans-Atlantic Slave Trade was able to exist because hard-hearted European sea captains were greedy for money and hard-hearted African rulers were greedy for power. When African

A typical slave ship

rulers traded people for European guns, they were able to conquer the people around them and increase their power. When European sea captains sold these people for money in the coastal ports of New York, Pennsylvania, Maryland, Virginia, North Carolina, South Carolina, Georgia, Central America, Cuba, Jamaica, the Bahamas, Puerto Rico, and South America, they made handsome profits.

Approximately one million (1,000,000) Africans arrived alive in the Americas during the slave trade. Most of these people worked as slaves in the sugar fields of Latin America. About 200,000 of them arrived alive in North America.

When African captives saw an opportunity to take over the ship and return home, they rebelled against their enslavers. One successful revolt occurred on the Spanish ship *Amistad*. It was led by a man named **Joseph Cinque**. To think that Cinque and his fellow captives were using sticks against people with guns is amazing to me.

In addition, the Africans on board the ship were from different areas of West Africa and spoke different languages. Can you imagine how difficult it was for Cinque to organize this uprising? He and his fellow freedom-seekers were strong, determined, and able to move quickly. After subduing their enslavers, Cinque and his men sailed the *Amistad* themselves.

When they reached the United States, all Africans on board the Amistad sued for their freedom. **President John Quincy Adams**, a European American, was the lawyer who represented the freedom-seekers in court. I like my brown skin because it reminds me of Cinque and all other Africans who tried to free themselves from bondage. What they did was awesome!

When African captives saw an opportunity to take over the ship and return home, they rebelled against their enslavers. One successful revolt occurred on the Spanish ship Amistad. It was led by a man named Joseph Cinque. To think that Cinque and his fellow captives were using sticks against people with guns is amazing to me.

The first Africans in the English colonies of North America were indentured servants who arrived in Jamestown, Virginia in 1619. This was one year before the Pilgrims sailed to Massachusetts on the Mayflower. These Africans worked without pay for seven years. Then they were free to work for themselves.

Many European Americans were indentured servants, too. They had chosen to be indentured in exchange for free passage to America. But they often ran away and blended in with other white-skinned people. Africans had not chosen to be servants. They were forcibly brought to America in chains. Because of their skin color, Africans could not blend in with Europeans so they could be easily identified as servants. Eventually, colonial legislative bodies changed the status of Africans from servant to slave. They enslaved all newly-arriving Africans for life.

After that, when Africans were brought to America in chains they were put on auction blocks and sold to Europeans who wanted enslaved laborers. At the auction blocks, men, women, and children were purchased as though they were horses.

African captives were given a few weeks to adjust to a new world of language, people, and food. They were given a new first name and eventually their last names were the enslavers' last names. They were not allowed to speak their African languages. Within four weeks, they were doing the work that built this country and produced America's early wealth.

They chopped down thick forests to clear the land for settlement. They opened mines and cultivated crops. In the North, Africans worked as house servants, farm hands, ship builders, dockworkers, and

African captives were given only a few weeks to adjust to a new world of language, people, and food. They were given a new first name and eventually their last names were the enslavers' last names. They were not allowed to speak their African languages. Within four weeks, they were doing the work that built this country and produced America's early wealth.

Farm owners and their families had comfortable homes that were dry and warm.

Slave cabins often leaked when it rained. They were too hot in the summer and too cold in the winter. They had pallets on the floor for sleeping.

crewmembers on cargo ships and whaling vessels. They also worked as tanners, carpenters, blacksmiths, and physician assistants. A few people of African descent served as printers, bookkeepers, and warehouse managers for enslavers.

In the United States, slavery was concentrated in the South because states in that section of the country had mild winters and long growing seasons. Unlike northern states, southern soil was fertile and it was suitable for large farms. Farm owners did not have to pay their enslaved laborers, so the owner of the farm was able to accumulate wealth. He and his family had a comfortable house to live in, good food to eat, medical care, educational opportunities, money saved, and money for leisure activities.

Enslaved people worked in the fields "from sun-up to sun-down."

The enslaved person was paid no money, so he had no advantages in life. His slave cabin often leaked when it rained. It was too hot in the summer, and too cold in the winter. Some cabins had planks for a floor but for others the bare dirt ground was the floor.

Enslaved people were given food the farm owner did not want. Their diet included the fatty parts of meat, lard (grease from pigs), and corn meal. They wore uncomfortable clothes and uncomfortable shoes. They had to work even when they were ill. Enslaved men could not protect themselves, and they could not protect their families. The enslaved person had no legal rights. Men, women, boys, and girls were completely owned by the enslaver and the law did not protect them from abuse. Instead, the law supported the enslaver in everything he did. In addition, the enslaver could sell enslaved people away from their families at any time. They could also be kidnapped by night raiders and sold to other plantations. As a result, enslaved people lived in fear. My brown skin reminds me of surviving sorrow and hard times. It also reminds me to be kind to others who are suffering.

There is nothing positive about owning a person or being owned by a person. Enslavers were not required to have any respect for enslaved people. In fact, they did not consider them people; they looked upon them as property. In court house records enslaved people were listed along with all other property that belonged to the enslaver:

*1 large table, 2 small tables, 4 beds, 3 lamps, 1 couch, 1 negro boy named Jim, 2 cows, 100 chickens, 2 negro girls of childbearing age, 3 heavy plows, 1 wagon, 1 old negress, etc.*

Enslaved people worked in the fields "from sun-up to sun-down." When their children were eight years old, they worked in the fields, too. Overseers beat the enslaved person who did not pick as much cotton as the enslaver thought he could pick. The beatings were painful, public, and humiliating. They let the enslaved people know that the enslavers were in total control.

The best way to avoid beatings was to do what the enslaver wanted you to do. In other words, be what the enslaver called a *good slave*, and never challenge the enslaver's authority. *Good slaves* kept their heads down and did not look enslavers in the eye. *Good slaves* did not show signs of intelligence. They did not ask questions. They did not speak up and express their opinions. In the presence of enslavers, *good slaves* acted as though they were mentally slow and confused. Being a *good slave* was to forget that you were human and to act as though you were another person's property. This is the exact opposite of what people were taught in West Africa.

●  ●  ●

# Precious Children,

While enslaved, African Americans had to become *good slaves* because they wanted to stay alive. In most of the situations you encounter today, you can stand with your head held high, look people in the eyes, and express your thoughts politely. You are free to be good people; you do not have to act like *good slaves*. You can live the truth the African ancestors taught – that no one on earth is better than you are.

However, there are some times when you might run into an ordinary citizen or even a police officer who does not have enough love in his or her heart to treat you right. When that person has a gun, you must be extremely careful. If that person calls you names and threatens you; if that person curses you and says something insulting about your family, you must do whatever is necessary to stay alive. Do not argue. Follow his or her directions immediately. In that moment of confrontation, our chief concern is that you survive.

Slavery was hard and it was cruel. To remain sane, African Americans held on to the belief that the future would be better than the present. They did not give up. Today's African Americans are the descendants of strong people who survived slavery. No matter what you are going through, keep believing that you will survive. And continue to believe that one day you will thrive. Look at your options. Do not give up. My brown skin reminds me of surviving and thriving. I like my brown skin: I like me.

Frederick Douglass (above), Henry "Box" Brown, William and Ellen Craft, and Harriet Tubman were enslaved people who found freedom. People were eager to hear their stories of slavery.

## CHAPTER 3

# I Like My Brown Skin Because...

## It Reminds Me That My Ancestors Created Personal Victories Over Slavery.

# I Am Victorious.

Enslaved people did not like slavery. They did whatever they could do to work against it. Some of them worked slowly to make sure they did not finish a job on schedule. Others pretended they did not understand instructions: they acted like they were clumsy and uncoordinated when using farm tools. When under the threat of being sold away from their family members, they faked illness and physical disabilities that kept other enslavers from buying them.

Many enslaved people conquered slavery psychologically (in their minds) and spiritually (in their hopes and prayers). They combined their African religious beliefs with the religion that was preached in the New World. They were especially attracted to the Old Testament stories of Daniel, David, Joshua, Jonah, Moses, and Noah. These biblical people had been in bondage, too, and they were rescued from their troubles in this world. Enslaved people sang songs called **Negro spirituals** that expressed their feelings and their belief in God. "Nobody Knows The Trouble I've Seen," "Swing Low, Sweet Chariot," and "Jesus Is A Rock In A Weary Land" are three of these spirituals. Many churches still sing these songs today. The belief that they, too,

When enslaved people were reading, another person stood at the cabin door to warn them if someone was coming.

would be delivered from slavery gave African Americans the will to live from one day to the next.

Other enslaved people fought against slavery by learning how to read and write. They knew education would empower them to help themselves. They would be able to read maps, newspapers, and signs.

They would be able to write passes that allowed them to travel from one location to another. A person who could read had a better chance of gaining freedom from slavery than a person who could not read.

Enslavers passed laws that punished people who taught African Americans to read, and an enslaved person with a book was beaten. Nonetheless, some enslavers' wives taught their cooks how to read recipes and taught their seamstresses how to read instructions. Some European children played "school" with their African playmates and taught them how to read. Some enslaved persons found work near open school windows and heard the lessons that were being taught to European American children.

## Precious Children,

Paying careful attention in school and learning everything you can possibly learn is one of the best things you can do for yourself. Do not be tricked into thinking that being a good student is wrong. Quite the contrary. West Africans valued education and African children spent their days learning. Being studious means you are smart and you will do well in life.

I like my brown skin because it reminds me of people who value education. They are people who like themselves. I value education. I like myself.

Harriet Tubman was a brilliant strategic planner. She led more than 300 people to freedom.

Armed with knowledge, a few African Americans started **secret "slave schools"** in their cabins at night. They knew they would be severely punished if caught, but they took that risk. They knew reading was the key to a better life.

Enslaved people also showed their discontent with slavery by running away. Enslavers and overseers tracked **freedom-seekers** down with dogs. After capture, the enslaver whipped the freedom-seeker in front of everybody. This public whipping was to show all African Americans what would happen to them if they tried to become free.

Perhaps the most famous freedom-seeker was **Harriet Tubman.** Not only did this brilliant, resourceful lady escape from slavery but she returned to the South nineteen times and led more than three hundred enslaved people to freedom. She was unselfish, she was brave, and she was a caring **strategic planner.** She had to get from a Southern state to a Northern state without being seen by a slave catcher. She had to make sure her "passengers" were quiet and children did not cry. She had to keep people from giving up and dropping out of the escape party. A reward of $40,000 was offered to anyone who captured her. But she outsmarted all the slave catchers. My brown skin reminds me of Harriet Tubman and I am always proud when I think of her. She was an absolutely phenomenal person.

**Henry "Box" Brown** was born into slavery in 1815 in Richmond, Virginia. After his wife and three children were sold away from him, he decided to attain freedom in an ingenious way. With the help of a free African American and a European American shoemaker, Henry Brown had himself mailed in a box to the Pennsylvania Anti-Slavery Society in Philadelphia. The box was 3 feet long, 2½ feet deep, and 2

Henry "Box" Brown had a very uncomfortable trip. Can you imagine being curled up in a box for twenty-seven hours? Gaining his freedom was worth the discomfort.

feet wide. Brown was curled up in that box for twenty-seven hours. He traveled by wagon, train, and steamboat until he reached Philadelphia. There, members of the **Pennsylvania Anti-Slavery Society** were waiting to open the box and welcome him to freedom. The Anti-Slavery Society was started by European Americans in the **Religious Society of Friends (Quakers)**.

**William and Ellen Craft** were an enslaved married couple in Macon, Georgia (1848) when they decided to escape from slavery. Ellen had very light skin and she was often mistaken for a European American. She made men's trousers for herself and pretended to be a wealthy European American man who was very ill. Her husband William pretended to be her enslaved helper on the train to Philadelphia. Ellen put her right arm in a sling so she would not have to sign her name, and she put bandages over the lower part of her face so she would not have to talk. She also pretended that she was hard of hearing. This caused people not to approach her with conversation. Upon reaching Philadelphia the Crafts presented themselves to the Anti-Slavery Society. This organization helped them start a new life as free people.

Another famous freedom-seeker was **Frederick Douglass.** After several beatings from his enslaver, he decided to fight back. When his enslaver was on the ground beaten and bloodied, Douglass ran away from the Maryland farm where he lived and made his way to Philadelphia. There, he joined the **American Abolition Society.** He was an exceptional orator (public speaker) and he talked about his slave experiences throughout the Northeastern section of the United States. He also traveled to England and spoke before huge crowds in that country. He wrote a book about his life and he published a newspaper called "The North Star." He even advised President Abraham Lincoln about issues that affected African Americans.

Hundreds of African Americans escaped from slavery, and Southern newspapers were full of notices offering rewards to slave-catchers who returned them to their enslavers:
- *1 negro fellow about 40 years old, very strong*
- *1 crippled black boy and his girl*
- *1 negress and her baby*

The last example of discontent with slavery was the slave rebellion. Slave rebellions frightened enslavers because they knew they were mistreating people and they expected some form of retaliation.

Nat Turner planning his rebellion

There were nine known slave revolts before the Civil War. One of these occurred in 1811 when a disciplined army of African American men began marching toward New Orleans. They freed all the enslaved people they saw, and it was several days before the state militia captured them.

**Nat Turner** led the most famous rebellion of all. It occurred in 1831 Virginia, and it lasted for forty-eight hours before being suppressed. Other potential rebellions were suppressed even before they took place. In 1822, **Denmark Vesey** planned a revolt in Charleston, South Carolina. An enslaved person revealed his plan to enslavers, and Vesey's revolt was stopped before it started. Enslaved people often revealed rebellions because they were afraid of the enslaver. When a revolt occurred the enslaver beat or killed every enslaved person who might possibly have known about the plan.

● ● ●

## Precious Children,

I like my brown skin because it reminds me to think about my situation and see what I can do to make it better. It reminds me to set a goal and to do something every day that gets me closer to that goal. It reminds me to make a plan and work that plan. My brown skin reminds me to have faith. It reminds me to keep hope alive even when my plans have been shattered. My brown skin reminds me to keep moving forward. It reminds me to keep thinking and keep trying. I like my brown skin: I like me.

## The Emancipation Proclamation
# September 22, 1862
(Selected Passages)

By the President: Abraham Lincoln

William H. Seward, Secretary of State

*That on the first day of January, in the year of our Lord one thousand, eight hundred and sixty-three, all persons held as slaves within any State, or designated part of a State, the people whereof shall then be in rebellion against the United States, shall be then, thenceforward, and forever free; and the Executive Government of the United States, including the military and naval authority thereof, will recognize and maintain the freedom of such persons, and will do no act or acts to repress such persons, or any of them, in any efforts they may make for their actual freedom.*

• • •

*And I further declare and make known that such persons of suitable condition will be received in the armed service of the United States to garrison forts, positions, stations, and other places, and to man vessels of all sorts in said service.*

## CHAPTER 4

# I Like My Brown Skin Because...

## It Reminds Me That There Are People Of All Colors Who Want To Do What Is Right.

# I Want To Do What Is Right.

As African Americans continued taking actions to end slavery, some European Americans started to help them. European Americans who belonged to the Religious Society of Friends organized the "**Underground Railroad.**" This was a series of homes in which freedom-seekers could rest while escaping from slavery. European Americans lived in most of the homes. They put themselves in danger of being arrested and jailed as they helped African Americans find freedom. They did this because they wanted to do what was right.

**William Lloyd Garrison, Elijah P. Lovejoy**, and **Wendell Phillips** also wanted to do the right thing. They were European Americans who wrote articles and published newspapers that opposed slavery. **Harriet Beecher Stowe** wrote about the hard lives of enslaved people in her book, *Uncle Tom's Cabin*. Many European Americans were disturbed by the conditions these writers described, and they took a stand against slavery. **People who wanted to end slavery were called abolitionists.**

Sojourner Truth                     Harriet Beecher Stowe

Another European American, **John Brown**, was a militant oppo-
nent of slavery. He led an attack on an arsenal in Harper's Ferry, West
Virginia, with hopes of freeing all enslaved people.

These European Americans joined **African American abolitionists** like **Harriett Tubman**, **Frederick Douglass**, **Henry Highland
Garnet**, **Solomon Northup**, **Martin Delaney**, **David Walker**, and
**Sojourner Truth (Isabella Baumfree)**. They wanted all people to be
free, and they wanted to do whatever it took to end slavery.

**Eventually, European Americans argued among themselves
over slavery.** Southerners wanted to expand slavery to the new terri-
tories and Northerners did not want it to be expanded. Northerners
supported legislation that favored factory owners and Southerners
supported legislation that favored farmers and agriculture. Both of

Henry Highland Garnet          William Lloyd Garrison

these factors led to tension between North and South. At one time, tempers flared so much that a South Carolina congressman used his metal-topped cane to beat up Massachusetts Senator Charles Sumner on the floor of the U.S. Senate.

**The Civil War** started after **Abraham Lincoln** was elected president of the United States. Southern state leaders thought he would end slavery, and they began to withdraw their states from the Union (secede). President Lincoln went to war to bring the seceded states back into the Union, and keep the United States together as one country. President Lincoln thought keeping the United States together was the right thing to do. He wanted to preserve this country as one nation.

Nearly 4,000,000 Americans served in the Civil War. **More than 175,000 People of Color served in the Union army.** Members of the

President Abraham Lincoln

Robert Smalls                                    USS Planter

54th Massachusetts Infantry Regiment, an all-black unit, were celebrated for their bravery at the Battle of Ft. Wagner in South Carolina.

People of Color also served in the Confederate (southern) armed services. Some were forced to serve, and others served because they feared change.

**Robert Smalls** was an enslaved man who was forced to pilot the *USS Planter* for the Confederate navy. In the early morning hours of May 13, 1862, Smalls and a crew of fellow enslaved men sneaked aboard the heavily-armed Planter, slipped it through the harbor, picked up family members at a designated point, and sailed into the open waters of the Atlantic Ocean. When he was beyond Confederate lines, Smalls raised a white flag of surrender and delivered the ship, its arms, and its passengers to the Union navy. **Robert Smalls had a**

**well-thought-out plan, he was brave, and he was determined.** What he did was incredible. He was later elected to the U.S. Congress.

In the summer of 1862, President Lincoln issued the **Emancipation Proclamation**. This proclamation freed enslaved people in the 11 states that had seceded from the Union. When they were freed, enslavers had to stop fighting and go home to work their own farms. As a result, the Emancipation Proclamation took manpower away from the Confederate army and helped bring the Civil War to an end.

The states that seceded are in red.

Senator Charles Sumner        Congressman Thaddeus Stevens

When it was finally over in 1865, slavery was abolished everywhere in the United States. The United States had chosen what was right.

A new day had dawned for African Americans.

They were legally free!!

At the end of the Civil War, there was still work to be done to protect the newly freed people. Massachusetts **Senator Charles Sumner** and Pennsylvania **Congressman Thaddeus Stevens** were European Americans who wanted to do what was right. They pushed their fellow congressmen to add the 13th, 14th, and 15th Amendments to the U.S. Constitution. The 13th Amendment (1865) abolished slavery everywhere in the United States, the 14th Amendment (1868) defined citizenship and included African Americans in that definition, and the 15th Amendment (1870) prevented states from denying the vote to any American male citizen. Right had triumphed over wrong. People of all colors had made this happen.

• • •

## Precious Children,

My brown skin reminds me that people of all colors can do what is right. All people can treat each other with love and kindness. Hatred and mistreatment do not have to exist in relationships. We can choose what is right in how we treat people.

I am grateful for African American abolitionists like Martin Delany, born a free man, who spent his career as a physician and a military officer. During the Civil War, he helped sick people of all colors. I am also grateful for Solomon Northup. Northup was a well-educated free man in Boston who was deceived, kidnapped, and sold into slavery in Louisiana. Upon being freed, he wrote *Twelve Years A Slave,* a book that detailed the brutal cruelty he had witnessed. His book prompted people to do the right thing and take a stand for freedom.

I am grateful for European American abolitionists like William Lloyd Garrison. He constantly condemned slavery in his newspaper called "The Liberator." I am grateful for Elijah P. Lovejoy who lost his life defending his warehouse from pro-slavery supporters who were trying to destroy his press and his abolitionist material. I am grateful for Wendell Phillips who was such an outstanding public speaker against slavery that he was called abolition's "Golden Trumpet."

I am grateful for Henry Highland Garnet, whose entire family escaped from slavery when he was nine years old. He became a minister and a militant abolitionist. I am also grateful for David Walker. As a free man he moved to Boston and opened a used clothing store but never forgot the chains he had seen and the cries of suffering he had heard while living in North Carolina. Like John Brown and Henry Highland Garnet, Walker wanted to end slavery by any means necessary.

Always remember that you have choices. You can choose to do what is right or you can choose to do what is wrong. I hope you choose what is right.

## What's So Great About Education?

Did you know that well-educated people live longer than people who are not well educated? In addition, they have fewer periods of sickness, and when they are ill they have better medical care. People who are well educated are more aware of what is going on around them and they have more choices of things to do. A well-educated person also has an easier time finding a job or changing jobs. They have more control over their jobs and more control over their lives.

As a group, well-educated people make more money than people who are not well educated, and they invest their money more wisely. Results: they have bigger bank accounts and bigger financial portfolios. They have bigger houses, they can travel more, and they have more access to people who can help them.

But the greatest thing about a good education is something rarely mentioned; namely that people who are well educated have more interesting lives than people who are not well educated. They have more to dream about, more to think about, more to talk about, more to imagine, more to create, more to appreciate, and more knowledge for problem-solving.

Pay attention and learn everything you are being taught in school. You will be glad you did.

## CHAPTER 5

# I Like My Brown Skin Because...

## It Reminds Me That My Ancestors Continued To Move Forward During Those Difficult Years After The Civil War.

# I Continue To Move Forward.

At the end of The Civil War, some Southern whites were angry because of the northern victory over Confederate troops. Many of them supported hate groups like the **Ku Klux Klan** and took out their anger on African Americans. The United States government temporarily stationed soldiers in the South to protect African Americans from these hate groups.

At this time, the newly-freed African Americans had no jobs, no money, and nowhere to live. Since landowners needed farm workers, they offered African Americans housing, tools for farming, and seeds for planting in exchange for work. At harvest time the workers would receive a share of the crop and they would repay the landowner for the housing and supplies they had received. This was called **sharecropping**. Sharecropping continued until southern cotton crops began to fail and the new automobile industry in the North began hiring African Americans as factory workers.

While stationed in the South, U.S. soldiers protected the right of African Americans to go to school. In 1865, the United States Congress established *The Bureau of Refugees, Freedmen and Abandoned Lands.* This Bureau opened schools for all people in the South, regardless of skin color. Four of today's most outstanding universities – Hampton, Howard, Atlanta, and Fisk – were founded by this agency. In all, the *Bureau of Refugees, Freedmen and Abandoned Lands* established 4,300 schools for people of all ages. Children and adults flocked to these schools. In 1870, their total enrollment was 250,000 students.

By 1900, there were two thousand African American college graduates. These graduates included **Dr. Daniel Hale Williams**, who became the first physician to successfully complete open-heart surgery on a patient; **Colonel Charles Young**, who earned a commission and a degree from West Point Military Academy; and **Charlotte Ray**, the first African American woman to earn a law degree. **Dr. Rebecca Lee, Dr. Rebecca Cole**, and **Dr. Susan McKinney** were among the first women of color to receive degrees from medical colleges.

**Mrs. Mary McLeod Bethune** and **Dr. Booker T. Washington** were the first two African Americans to become college presidents. Dr. Washington was president of **Tuskegee Institute** in Alabama, and Mrs. Bethune was co-founder and president of **Bethune-Cookman College** in Daytona Beach, Florida. When she was five-years old, Mary McLeod (Bethune) walked five miles to school everyday. At home in the evenings, she taught her parents and her siblings what she had learned. Young Mary often talked about building a school for children. As an adult, she started Bethune Academy with just six children. Each year she added another grade to her school. In later years, she

People of all ages learning in a school established by the *Bureau of Refugees, Freedmen and Abandoned Lands*

Mrs. Mary McLeod Bethune

merged Bethune Academy with Cookman College. Building a school was Mrs. Bethune's goal. She moved forward toward her goal until she accomplished it. Bethune-Cookman University is still educating young people today.

My brown skin reminds me of the brilliance of Dr. Booker T. Washington. He was born into slavery but after emancipation he attended Hampton Institute to learn vocational skills. When he was president of Tuskegee Institute, his students majored in agriculture, mechanical engineering, veterinary science, masonry, carpentry, sewing, tailoring, nursing, homebuilding, culinary skills, and other programs that prepared them for jobs that were needed. I am proud of Dr. Washington's accomplishments and I am proud of Mrs. Bethune's accomplishments. I'm glad I look like them.

Dr. Booker T. Washington

Hampton Institute students finishing the interior of a building they have constructed

# Precious Children,

When I think about my brown skin, I think about the importance of taking advantage of opportunities. After slavery, my ancestors went to school in droves. They went in old, faded clothing. They went with bare feet. Even a ten-mile walk did not stop them from going to school. They paid attention to the teacher and they did their homework. They wanted knowledge, and they valued education. As a result, they improved their lives.

I like what my ancestors did. They had a goal, and I want you to have a goal, too. Your goal right now is to learn everything good that you can learn. Keep a knowledge book. Every evening write in this book what you know today that you did not know yesterday. What you know will be extremely helpful to you in life. My brown skin reminds me of setting a goal, making a plan to achieve that goal, and following that plan. I like my brown skin: I like me.

Benjamin Banneker, a mathematical genius, correctly predicted the appearance of comets and eclipses. He helped plan the city of Washington, D.C.

## CHAPTER 6

## It Reminds Me That Success Can Be Found In All Situations.

# I Am Successful.

When I think of African Americans who were successful in all kinds of conditions and all kinds of places, my brown skin makes me glad. I smile about **James Forten** who became a very successful sail maker after the Revolutionary War. He made sails for ships and he built one of the largest and most profitable sail-making businesses on the East Coast. When he died in 1842, Forten left an estate of $100,000, a great fortune for that time.

I smile about **Dr. James Derham** who was encouraged to become a physician by the Philadelphia doctor who enslaved him. Derham worked as a doctor's assistant until he purchased his freedom in 1790. He continued to study medicine and he was highly regarded for his knowledge. I can imagine he felt a real sense of pride as leading doctors consulted with him about their patients. Dr. Derham was called in to examine Benjamin Franklin during his final illness.

I smile about **Richard Allen**, an African American who attended St. George's Methodist Episcopal Church in Philadelphia. In that church, People of Color had to sit in the back of the Sunday school classrooms, they were served communion only after all Europeans were served,

Jim Beckwourth

and the kneeling bench where they prayed had a "Colored" section and a "White" section. I find it difficult to believe that people had color in their minds as they prayed, but I guess they did. Allen grew tired of this discrimination. In 1787, he led African Americans from St. George's in protest. These protesters eventually founded the **African Methodist Episcopal Church**. In that same period of time, **George Liele** was establishing the First African Baptist Church in Savannah, Georgia.

I also smile when I think of **Benjamin Banneker**. He was a brilliant African American mathematician and astronomer who correctly predicted the appearance of comets and eclipses. He also constructed the first clock in America that contained all American-made parts. In 1791, President George Washington appointed Banneker to the commission that planned the city of Washington, D.C. When the leader of the project, Pierre L'Enfant, got angry and went home to France, he took the written plans with him. Fortunately Banneker had memorized the plans and he drew them again.

I'm glad President Washington did not let color get in the way of talent. When discrimination keeps people out of any position or organization, the entire society suffers. People of all colors have brains, talents, personalities, and abilities. All people are needed.

**Jim Beckwourth** was an African American who became a tribal chief of the Crow Indians. In 1850, he discovered a pass through the Sierra Nevada Mountains. *Beckwourth Pass* made it easier for people to get to the territory west of that mountain range.

I have read about the relations between Indians and African Americans in the United States. I have also heard about these relationships in my own family. Both groups felt mistreated by European Americans and they befriended each other. When Africans ran away from slavery, they often found shelter with nearby Indians. It was not uncommon for Indians and Africans to marry each other.

My brown skin reminds me of other brown people who improved their own lives and made great contributions to this nation. I enjoy reading about them, I enjoy talking about them, and I enjoy writing about them. Does my brown skin make me sad?? No way – my brown skin makes me smile.

**Bridgett "Biddy" Mason** is one of my favorite people in history. She was born into slavery in 1818. When her enslavers moved to California, they took her with them. California was a free state so Miss Mason sued in court for her freedom and won. In Los Angeles, Miss Mason worked as a nurse and a midwife. She saved her money and was one of the first African Americans to purchase land in that city. Her land investments made her wealthy and she amassed a fortune of $300,000. "Biddy" Mason was very kind. She often fed and sheltered people who were having a hard time in life. She also visited people in prison. Since there was no elementary school Children of Color were allowed to attend, Miss Mason donated the money to build a school for them. In 1872, Bridgett "Biddy" Mason helped establish the First African Methodist Episcopal Church in Los Angeles. I like this lady. She is one of my role models.

Miss "Biddy" Mason was smart, and she took advantage of opportunties. She was kind and she had a spirit of doing what was right. Does my brown skin make me sad? Oh no, when I look at my brown skin and think of Biddy Mason's brown skin, I smile.

Miss Bridgett "Biddy" Mason

One of the most interesting stories of African American settlement in the West is the story of **Barney Ford.** He was a man who looked for opportunities and considered his options. Barney Ford was born into slavery in 1822. He was hired out to work on a Mississippi River cargo boat. While this boat was docked in Illinois (a free state), Ford declared himself free and his freedom was recognized by law.

Later, **Ford and his wife Julia** decided to go to California and search for gold. They traveled by ship around Cape Horn and when they got to Nicaragua, and saw business opportunities, they settled in that country. There, they started a successful hotel and a restaurant. When a civil war broke out in Nicaragua, the Fords returned to the United States and settled in Colorado. Barney Ford wanted to search for gold. But since he was of African descent, he was not allowed to stake a claim for gold in his name. Instead, he made money by starting a barbershop, a restaurant, and a hotel. By 1875, the Ford family was one of the richest families in Denver.

The largest group of African Americans in the West were soldiers who had fought in the Civil War. Their job was to protect western set-tlers. Plains Indians referred to these African American soldiers as "**Buffalo Soldiers**" because of their brown skin, their curly hair, their strength, and their courage. This was a term of great respect. Plains Indians used the buffalo for food, shelter, and clothing. The buffalo was their source of survival.

Civilian People of Color worked in the cattle business and they were some of the best **cowboys** on the range. They were also active

Nat Love was an outstanding cowboy. One-fourth of all cowboys in the United States were African Americans.

in rounding up horses, breaking wild horses, and taming horses. The most well known cowboys were **Nat Love, Bose Ikard, Bass Reeves, Bill Pickett**, and **Addison Jones**. One-fourth of all cowboys in the United States were African Americans.

As a child I watched "cowboy movies" on television. There was never any mention of brown-skinned cowboys. People who looked like me were not included in the movies.

In the wide-open spaces of the West, there was certainly discrimination but skin color was not as important as abilities. A person's skills with a lariat, a rifle, a pistol, a frying pan, and a horse were what allowed that person to survive. In demonstrating these abilities, Americans of color certainly made their marks.

**Nat Love** was nicknamed "Deadwood Dick" after he won contests for best roper, best colt .45 shooter, and best rifle shooter in Deadwood, South Dakota on July 4, 1876. **Pinto Jim, Bronco Jim Davis,** and **Bill Pickett** (top bulldogger) were other African Americans who participated and excelled in western rodeos.

● ● ●

# Precious Children,

I smile about the accomplishments of people like James Forten, Dr. James Derham, Richard Allen, Benjamin Banneker, James Beckwourth, and Miss "Biddy" Mason who made tremendous accomplishments against tremendous odds.

I also smile about the fact that life always comes with choices. If one thing does not work out the way you want it to, do not despair. Look for something else. Richard Allen certainly looked for something else when he decided he would not put up with discrimination in church. In looking for something else, he started a church that did not practice segregation.

I really like the way Barney and Julia Ford went to "Plan B" when "Plan A" did not work for them. Always keep your eyes open for positive opportunities. Your current situation does not have to be permanent.

I am impressed with the Buffalo Soldiers, and with the great job African American cowboys did on the Western range. My brown skin reminds me of my ability to practice and sharpen my skills in every arena. It reminds me of my ability to excel. My brown skin reminds me that I can compete, and I can be a winner. I can be successful in life. I like my brown skin: I like me.

Granville T. Woods

## CHAPTER 7

# I Like My Brown Skin Because...

## It Reminds Me Of African American Inventors And Entrepreneurs At The Turn Of The 20th Century.

# I Am Creative.

My brown skin makes me smile when I think of inventors with brown skin. **Jan Ernst Matzeliger, Granville T. Woods, Lewis Latimer, Garrett Morgan, and Elijah McCoy all** had brown skin.

In 1883, **Jan Ernst Matzeliger** invented a "lasting machine" that attached soles to shoes. Before his invention, the cobbler who did the attachment by hand could only produce 50 pairs of shoes per day. With Matzeliger's "lasting machine," one cobbler could produce 700 pairs of shoes per day.

**Granville T. Woods** (1856-1910) invented the "Troller." The "Troller" provided perfect contact between the electric street-car and the overhead wires that powered the streetcar. Because of Woods' invention, streetcars were later called "trolley cars." Woods also invented the induction telegraph system. This system allowed train conductors to avoid crashes by informing each other of their locations. His third rail electrical system is still being used in New York City subways. Woods' other inventions included automatic air brakes, automatic circuit breakers, and electromagnetic brakes.

Lewis Latimer

**Lewis Latimer** (1848-1928) was making his scientific contributions at this time, too. Working with Thomas Edison, Latimer invented the filament for the electric light bulb. In his association with Alexander Graham Bell, Latimer drew the blueprints for the first telephone.

**Garrett Morgan** was a successful inventor and community activist whose parents had been enslaved. Among Morgan's inventions are the **gas mask** (US patent 1,113,675) that was used during World War I to protect soldiers from chlorine gas fumes and a patent for a **traffic signal with three positions** (US patent 1,475,024). The key innovation of Morgan's traffic signal over earlier versions was the introduction of a third position to give drivers a warning to slow down (this was the precursor to the "yellow" signal).

**Elijah McCoy** was born free in Colchester, Ontario, Canada after his parents escaped to that country through the "Underground Railroad." He invented an automatic lubricator for oiling the steam engines of locomotives and ships. His lubricator allowed trains to run faster with less need to stop for oil. Between 1872 and 1920, Elijah McCoy received

57 patents on systems he invented that automatically oiled machinery.

The complete list of African American scientists who received patents for their inventions and discoveries is too long to include in this book. However, we will mention a few more to give you a general picture of their expertise. In 1821, **Thomas L. Jennings** became the first African American to file a U.S. patent when he invented a **dry cleaning process** called dry scouring (US patent X3306); **Henry T. Blair** invented the **seed planter machine** for planting corn in 1834 (US patent X8447); **George T. Sampson** invented the **clothes dryer** (US patent 476,416); **Thomas J. Marshall** invented the **fire extinguisher sprinkling system** (US patent 125,063); **Charles B. Brooks** received a patent for a **self-propelled street sweeper** (US patent 556,711); **Charles Beckley** invented a **folding chair** (US patent 4,046,417); **John A. Burr** invented an **improved lawn mower** that was less likely to get clogged than traditional ones (US patent 624,749); **Otis F. Boykin** invented a **wire type resistor** that enabled precise resistance control – his resistor was used in hundreds of electronics and computing devices including pacemakers; **John Stanard** invented an **oil stove** (US patent 413,689) as well as an **improved refrigerator** (US patent 455,891); **Richard Spikes** had several inventions including an improved **automatic gearshift for automobiles** in 1931 that he licensed for $100,000 (US patent 1,889,814); **Frederick McKinley Jones** invented a **refrigeration system for trucks** (US patent 2,475,841) and an improved **thermostat** (US patent 2,926,005); **Lloyd Hall** made several important **discoveries related to food preservation** (such as US patent 2,107,697) and received over 100 US and foreign patents; **Alexander Miles** received a patent in 1887 for a **system to automatically open and close elevators doors** (US patent 371,207); and

Madam C. J. Walker (Sarah Breedlove), inventor and a businesswoman.

**James B. Huntley** received a patent for a **portable, self-contained fire escape** mechanism (US patent 3,880,255). In 1885, **Sarah Elizabeth Goode** was the first African American woman to receive a patent with her invention of a "**folding cabinet bed**," a forerunner of the convertible sleeper sofa; **Hubert Julian** received a patent in 1925 for an **airplane safety device** (US patent 1,379,264); and **James Sloan Adams** received a patent for a **means of propulsion for airplanes** (US patent 1,356,329).

I smile when I think of brilliant African American inventors and business owners like **Madam C. J. Walker (Sarah Breedlove)**. She was an inventor and an entrepreneur. She became a multimillionaire when she produced hair and facial products for African American women. Mrs. Walker was one of the first African American women to amass $1,000,000 (one million dollars). By 1900, there were four **banks** owned by African Americans. **Mrs. Maggie Lena Walker**, of Richmond, Virginia, was the first woman of any color to be president of a bank. She founded the **St. Luke Penny Savings Bank** in 1903.

**The Atlanta Life Insurance Company** and **The North Carolina**

# *Precious Children,*

I am always interested in the things people invent.

Often the invention is something simple and fairly obvious

that makes me say, "Why didn't I think of that?" Put your

thinking caps on. What would you like to invent? What needs

to be invented, or what needs to be improved on? What

needs to be made easier? To increase the gross national

product of the United States we need more inventions to sell

abroad. President Barack Obama has challenged all of us to

invent something. What ideas do you have? What would you

like to invent?

**Mutual Life Insurance Company** were two of the eighty **insurance companies** established by African Americans before 1929.

Let me mention just a few other businesses owned by African Americans at the turn of the 20th century. In 1883, **Charles H. James** traded household goods (pots, pans, dishes, cups, soap, lamps, small tables, irons, etc.) for vegetables and fruits from farmers who had gardens and fruit trees. He sold the vegetables and fruits to coal miners who did not have gardens, and used the cash to buy other household goods that he traded for produce. Then he sold these fruits and vegetables to coal miners. He continued doing this until his earnings were enough for him to save a handsome profit. His sons expanded the business and by 1918 the James Produce Company was the largest wholesale food distributor in West Virginia. As the 20th century turned into the 21st, the C.H. James Company had a $1 million contract to supply food to the U.S. Dept. of Veterans Affairs, a $2 million yearly contract to supply goods to the U.S. Dept of Agriculture, and a $9.6 million contract to furnish food to the military during Operation Desert Storm. When we eat at McDonald's, Taco Bell, and Wendy's, we are eating lettuce and onion supplied by the C.H. James Company.

Arthur George Gaston was another outstanding businessman who made his mark near the middle of the 20th century. After serving in World War I, he worked in Alabama coal mines. He made lunches and sold them to fellow coal miners. When he noticed that many of the coal miners did not have life insurance, he started the Booker T. Washington Insurance Company. When the miners needed extra money he loaned them money at 25% interest. With his profits, he built The Citizens Federal Savings and Loan Association, a very successful bank. In Birmingham, he built the only hotel in Alabama that allowed African Americans as guests. When he died in 1995 at 103 years old, Gaston's net worth was $130,000,000.

The Greenwood section of Tulsa, Oklahoma was a bustling commercial section of African American businesses in the early 1900s. It had 30 African American-owned grocery stores, 21 restaurants, 21 churches, two movie theaters, banks, pharmacies, libraries, real estate offices, barber shops, beauty parlors, buildings that housed two newspapers (*The Tulsa Star* and *The Oklahoma Sun*), a hospital, and beautiful houses belonging to African American doctors, lawyers, and businessmen. There were only two airports in the state of Oklahoma but six of

Greenwood's wealthy African American residents owned airplanes. People of Color were also able to establish thriving business communities in Atlanta and Durham, North Carolina. Some European Americans were envious of, and angry about, African American prosperity. In 1923 police officers did not stop an angry European American mob from burning the Greenwood section of Tulsa to the ground. This did not happen in Atlanta and Durham.

**President Calvin Coolidge said, "The business of America is business." What business would you like to start? Think of how you can start a business that is needed in your community.**

• • •

## Precious Children,

My brown skin reminds me of brilliant brown inventors and brilliant brown entrepreneurs who understood the basic principals of financial literacy. They studied the market to see what was needed. Then they worked, saved, and invested their money in well-respected businesses that they owned. Many of them made a good living for their families, and some of them became wealthy. I like the way these brown people operated. I like my brown skin: I like me.

## Fighting for One's Country

African Americans have participated in every war the United States has ever fought:

The French and Indian War

The Revolutionary War

The War of 1812

The Mexican-American War

The Spanish-American War

World War I

World War II

The Korean War

The Vietnam War

The First Gulf War

The War in Iraq

The War in Afghanistan

## CHAPTER 8

## I Like My Brown Skin Because...

### It Reminds Me That People Who Looked Like Me Helped Win Every War The United States Has Ever Fought.

# I Am A Loyal American.

Let's look at just three American wars, starting with the **Revolutionary War** that made America a free and independent country. In 1770 an African American named **Crispus Attucks** was the first to die at the hand of the British in a confrontation between young men and British soldiers that became known as the Boston Massacre. After General George Washington promised that enslaved people would be free if they joined his militia, more than **5,000 Africans** served in the Continental Army. They fought in every crucial battle of the Revolutionary War: from Lexington, to Concord, to Brandywine, to Saratoga, and to the final battle at Yorktown where the British surrendered.

**Peter Salem, Job Potomea, Isaiah Barjonah,** and **Cuff Whitemore** were four black Minutemen who responded to Paul Revere's call to fight the British in April of 1775 at the beginning of the Revolutionary War.

Peter Salem stopping the British Major General Pitcairn at the Battle of Bunker Hill

Peter Salem also played an important role at the **Battle of Bunker Hill** when he shot the British Major General John Pitcairn as the general was rallying his troops. Today his gun is displayed at Bunker Hill with a sign that says, "Gun belonged to Peter Salem, a Colored man who carried it at Lexington, Concord, and Bunker Hill, and with it shot Major General Pitcairn."

Before the United States entered **World War I**, men and women of color worked in the new factories that produced war-related materials for the allies. When the U.S. Congress declared war on Germany, African American soldiers fought in Europe. The **92nd Infantry Division** was

Henry Johnson

a segregated unit composed entirely of African American soldiers. This division arrived in France in June of 1918, and remained under heavy enemy fire until the end of the war. In the words of General John J. Pershing (commander of the allied forces), "This division was one of the best in the Allied Expeditionary Force."

The entire **369th Infantry** won the French *Croix de Guerre* for gallantry after being under continuous enemy fire for a record-breaking period of 191 days. **Henry Johnson** and **Needham Roberts,** two African American soldiers in the 369th Infantry, performed one of the most sensationally heroic feats of **World War I**. In May of 1918, they were attacked by approximately twenty

German soldiers referred to the 369th Infantry as "Harlem Hellfighters" because they were so tough in battle. None of the 369th was ever captured, they never lost a trench, and they never lost an inch of ground that was under their command.

German troops. Although badly wounded, Johnson and Roberts fought back bravely and made the enemy soldiers retreat. This great deed prevented their entire unit from being killed. Both Johnson and Roberts were awarded the highest military honor bestowed by the French government. However, discrimination kept them from being honored by the United States until May of 2015, nearly one hundred years after showing such military commitment and bravery. At that time Henry Johnson was awarded the Medal of Honor by President Barack Obama. Since Johnson and all of his relatives had died, the Command Sergeant of the New York National Guard accepted the honor. I am sorry that Henry Johnson was not given this medal when he was alive as his European American counterparts were. It was his and I know he would have been proud.

Just before the U.S. entered **World War II**, two African American research scientists, **Dr. George Washington Carver** and **Dr. Charles Richard Drew**, made remarkable breakthroughs that helped the allied war effort.

Dr. Carver was a chemist who developed plant products that help us in our everyday lives. He produced an inexpensive soybean plastic that could replace metal in domestic vehicles. **Dr. Carver and Henry Ford**, president of the Ford Motor Company, made a joint announcement of Dr. Carver's product in 1942. Soon thereafter, automobiles began rolling off assembly lines with important parts made of soybean plastic. This left more metal for war equipment.

Carver also experimented with peanuts and sweet potatoes. He made peanut butter, a meat substitute, instant coffee, caramel, mayonnaise, lotion, dyes, paints, rubbing oil, linoleum, and printers ink.

George Washington Carver

Dr. Carver had a passion for agriculture, and he became an expert on southern crops. What do you enjoy thinking about in your spare time? That is your passion. Read about it, learn everything about it, and love it. Your passion will lead you to a wonderful life.

**Dr. Charles Richard Drew** helped save thousands of lives during World War II after he discovered a method for processing and preserving blood plasma (blood without cells). Plasma lasts much longer than whole blood, making it possible to be stored for longer periods of time.

Prior to the United States entering WWII, Dr. Drew was selected to set up and administer the U.S. Blood for Britain Project. This was the world's first blood plasma bank. It eventually became the American Red Cross Blood Bank. Because of Dr. Drew, when wounded soldiers arrived at military hospitals, blood was readily available for those who needed it.

Dr. Charles R. Drew

Approximately one million African Americans served their country in **World War II.** This number included **General Benjamin O. Davis, Sr.,** the first Person of Color to receive the rank of general in the United States Army. General Davis wanted to be a soldier so much that he moved his age up a year when he joined the army. He served a total of 50 years in the military, and he fought in four wars. He was awarded the Bronze Star Medal, and the Distinguished Service Medal. He eventually became an advisor for the military on race relations. In this capacity he pushed for full integration of the armed forces.

General Davis's son, **General Benjamin O. Davis, Jr.,** was a graduate of West Point Academy. During his entire four years there, none of the other students ever spoke to him. They were hoping their silent treatment would cause him to leave. But Davis stayed. He became commander of the **Tuskegee Airmen,** and he was the first African

American general in the Air Force. The Tuskegee Airmen were 994 pilots of color who flew escort planes for American bombers over Austria, Poland, Czechoslovakia, Hungary and Germany. Their job was to destroy enemy planes before they could attack U.S. bombers.

Some military officials hoped these Tuskegee Airmen would be failures. But quite the opposite was true. The Tuskegee Airmen were the best escort pilots in the military. They were so good that

General Benjamin O. Davis, Sr.

they had one of the lowest loss records of all the escort fighter groups. Bomber pilots constantly asked the Tuskegee Airmen to escort their airplanes. Even the enemy German pilots commented on how good they were at shooting down German planes. Eighty-two Tuskegee Airmen were awarded the Distinguished Flying Cross.

In addition to the Army, African Americans also excelled in the Navy. An African American man named **Dorrie Miller** earned the Navy Cross Award for shooting down enemy aircraft at Pearl Harbor. Discrimination did not allow Miller to receive training as a gunner. But, during the Pearl Harbor assault when Miller realized that the European American gunner near him had been wounded, he manned an anti-aircraft gun (with no training) and helped repel the Japanese attack.

• • •

The Tuskegee Airmen were 994 pilots of color who flew escort planes for American bombers over Austria, Poland, Czechoslovakia, Hungary and Germany. Their job was to destroy enemy planes before they could attack U.S. bombers. They were among the best escort pilots in the military.

# Precious Children,

Sometimes people say something is true that is really not true at all. In the 1930s, American military officials said African Americans did not have the ability to fly an airplane. The Tuskegee Airmen put an end to that false idea when their flying skills and bravery made them among the best of all the World War II escort fighter pilots.

No matter what negative comments others make about you, don't let their thinking stop you from reaching your goals and your full potential. Don't let anyone stop you from being the wonderful person you were meant to be.

I like my brown skin because it reminds me of the Tuskegee Airmen. My brown skin also reminds me of Crispus Attucks; Peter Salem; Robert Smalls; Henry Johnson; Needham Roberts; Dr. George Washington Carver; Dr. Charles R. Drew; General B.O. Davis Sr.; Dorrie Miller; General B.O. Davis Jr., my own father, a 2nd Lieutenant who served in Italy during World War II; and every other African American who helped win American wars. I like my brown skin: I like me.

## CHAPTER 9

# I Like My Brown Skin Because...

## It Reminds Me Of My Ancestors' Inner Power To Prevent Discrimination From Defeating Them.

# I Am A Winner.

Most European Americans did not want African Americans to have the same rights, privileges, and opportunities that *they* enjoyed. Therefore, they convinced themselves of a lie. Their lie was that African Americans were not as good as European Americans. To keep that lie strong, they created a social system that required separate facilities for people of different colors.

Under the **"Jim Crow"** laws, everything from drinking fountains and schools, to libraries, hospitals, cemeteries, and swimming pools were labeled "White" or "Colored." The "White" facilities were always nicer than the "Colored" ones. African Americans were arrested and jailed for using a restroom or drinking fountain that was not assigned to them.

**Segregation** and **discrimination** were as much alive in the North as they were in the South. African Americans could only live in neighborhoods set aside for them, they could only sit in the balconies of movie theaters, and they could not eat at public lunch counters. They could not work as sales clerks in downtown stores, most banks did not lend money to them, and they were hired only for the least desirable jobs.

Dr. W.E.B. DuBois and Oswald Garrison Villard founded The NAACP.

Segregation was an extreme insult to African Americans. After all, they had done just as much to build this country as other Americans. They had worked hard during times of peace, and they had fought and died in American wars.

When waves of European immigrants began coming to the United States after the Civil War, they were given privileges that were not given to African Americans. These "white privileges" included police protection, good-paying jobs, housing, education, loans from banks for starting businesses, investment opportunities, and the presumption of innocence in courts of law.

Let's look at how these **"white privileges"** helped European Americans to achieve success. With good-paying jobs, European Americans could purchase a house that would increase in value. Their children had access to quality schools. They could invest in land, stocks, big insurance policies, and businesses. Good investments allowed European American parents to leave an inheritance to their children. As a result, their children had even more privileges than the parents had. This continued from generation to generation, and it is one of the reasons that white families today have more accumulated wealth than black families.

In 1909 a group of African Americans, led by **Dr. W. E. B. DuBois**, and a group of European Americans, led by **Oswald Garrison Villard** (grandson of the abolitionist William Lloyd Garrison), established the *National Association for the Advancement of Colored People* (The NAACP). One year later, **The National Urban League** was organized. The goal of the NAACP was to end discrimination in American public life through the courts. The Urban League was dedicated to helping new city dwellers find suitable housing, job training, and wholesome recreation. Both the NAACP and the Urban League had big tasks before them.

In addition, there were other African Americans who spoke out against actions and conditions that were not right. They were ordinary people who told the truth about the impact of powerful people's decisions on their lives. This is called speaking truth to power. **Ida B. Wells-Barnett** was one of these people. She was born into slavery, she was a founding member of the NAACP, she supported voting for women, and she was a journalist. She also published a newspaper. As a journalist, Mrs. Wells wrote articles that condemned the lynching of African Americans. Between 1877 and 1910, approximately 3,000 People of Color were lynched (purposely killed) by European American mobs and no one was ever charged with a crime.

During World War I, African Americans fought and died to help "make the world safe for democracy" in Europe. When they came home, they wanted to enjoy democracy in the United States. They began to express themselves in new ways. In fact, they referred to themselves as **"New Negroes,"** and they took actions they had previously been reluctant to take.

● They stepped up their efforts to vote even though they knew they could be beaten, fired from their jobs, or killed for voting in some parts of the country.

● When attacked by mobs, they defended themselves.

● They insisted on spending their money with businesses that hired African Americans. Their slogan was, "Don't buy where you cannot work."

Brave people like Mrs. Ida B. Wells stood up to people in power who unjustly harmed African Americans. She "spoke truth to power."

Paul Robeson

● They brilliantly expressed their feelings in novels, poetry, theater, and music (jazz). Their expressions were known as the *Harlem Renaissance* (named after a neighborhood in New York City). Writer **Langston Hughes**, poets **Claude McKay** and **James Weldon Johnson**, actor **Paul Robeson**, and musicians **Louis Armstrong**, **Bessie Smith**, and **Duke Ellington** are but a few of the outstanding people who shared their talents during the *Harlem Renaissance*.

Paul Robeson was a scholar (valedictorian of his college class at Rutgers University), an athlete, an actor, a lawyer, a singer, and a political activist. He is called a political activist because he spoke out against segregation and discrimination in America. A political activist is a person who has an impact on political policy even though he does not hold a political office. Through his criticism of segregation and discrimination, Robeson helped America achieve its goals as a nation.

When World War II began in Europe, The United States used tax money to make weapons for England, France, and other allies. Ninety percent of the companies making these weapons had discrimination policies that prevented the hiring of African Americans.

**A. Phillip Randolph** sought to right that wrong. He proposed a March on Washington of 100,000 people to protest the fact that the American government ("the arsenal of democracy") was denying democracy to its own people and allowing this discrimination to take place. Randolph set July 1, 1941 as the date for the March.

**President Franklin Delano Roosevelt** knew this discrimination was wrong. He also knew that a march would be embarrassing to the United States because it would expose American wrong-doing to the rest of the world. To prevent the march, Roosevelt issued **"Executive Order 8802."** "Executive Order 8802" directed vocational training to be given without regard to skin color, and it declared that all future defense contracts should include non-discrimination clauses. "Executive Order 8802" also established a **Fair Employment Practice Committee** to see that the first two ideas were carried out.

● ● ●

# Precious Children,

My brown skin reminds me of Dr. W.E.B. DuBois who, with Oswald Garrison Villard, established The National Association for the Advancement of Colored People. My brown skin reminds me of Mrs. Ida B. Wells Barnett who continued to write articles against lynching even when her life was threatened.

My brown skin reminds me of "New Negroes" who marched against injustices, expressed themselves in music and writing, and spoke out against lynching. They made the United States of America a better nation for me, for you, and for everybody else. I am proud of these brown people and the European Americans who joined their protests.

My brown skin reminds me of Asa Phillip Randolph, a courageous man who thought critically, and planned a program of action that led to positive changes in America. When he presented his plan to President Roosevelt, he was speaking truth to power. He told the truth about the impact of powerful people's decisions on other people's lives. In this case it was the impact of African Americans not being hired in companies that had government contracts. I am proud of how my brave brown-skinned ancestors spoke truth to power. I like my brown skin: I like me.

A. Phillip Randolph spoke truth to power. He knew that demonstrations against injustices would make the United States a better nation.

## Other People Have Suffered from Discrimination, Too.

African American men and women are not the only people who suffered from discrimination in the United States. Native American people, Irish people, Italian people, Polish people, Jewish people, Catholics, Asians, and European American women are among others who have been hurt by discrimination.

There was a period in American history when advertisements for jobs included the words, "No Irish Need Apply." Some European Americans whose ancestors came here from England, France, and Germany did not want descendants of Italian, Irish, and Polish people to live in the same neighborhoods they lived in. Written and signed agreements, called restrictive covenants, prevented Jews and Catholics from living in certain areas of major cities.

All women regardless of color have suffered from discrimination in the United States. Women were not always allowed to go to school, women were not always hired for employment, and women could not always vote. In fact, women did not receive the vote until 1920. Even in the 21st century, some businesses have discriminated against women. They have not paid women as much money as they have paid men for doing the same job.

Discrimination is ugly wherever it exists!

## CHAPTER 10

# I Like My Brown Skin Because...

## It Reminds Me Of The Moral Strength Displayed By African Americans As The United States Was Being Desegregated.

# I Have Moral Strength, Too.

For years, African American soldiers had been insisting on the desegregation of America's **military forces** because it was ridiculous and impractical for people fighting on the same side and for the same cause to be divided. Three years after the end of World War II, **President Harry S. Truman** issued **"Executive Order 9981."** This order desegregated the American armed forces. In future wars, Americans of all colors would fight in units together as one nation.

Individuals of color have always made significant contributions in all areas of human accomplishments. But it was in the field of **sports** that African Americans became most visible and most acknowledged for their achievements. In track and field, **Jesse Owens** won four gold medals at the 1936 Olympics in Berlin. **Jack Johnson** and Joe Louis were heavy weight boxing champions. African Americans were extremely proud of **Joe Louis** in 1938 when he knocked out the German boxer Max Schmeling. Adolf Hitler, Chancellor of Germany, had bragged about the superiority of Aryans over all other people. Joe Louis's rights and lefts to Schmeling caused the chancellor to cease his talk. Regardless of what Hitler said, all people were human beings, no more and no less.

Baseball was America's favorite sport but People of Color were not hired for national teams. As a result, they formed their own athletic teams and competed with each other. The **"Negro Leagues"** were filled with outstanding players and outstanding stories are told about them. **Leroy "Satchel" Paige** pitched the baseball so fast that the batter could not see it coming across the plate. **Josh Gibson** once hit a homerun into the right-field upper deck of Yankee Stadium with one hand. A tall tale is even told about Gibson hitting a ball in Pittsburgh so hard, so high, and so fast that it landed in Philadelphia the next day, some four hundred miles away.

Segregation in sports began to crumble when **Jackie Robinson** was offered a contract to play major league baseball with the Brooklyn Dodgers. From his first day in the system, people were mean to Jackie Robinson. Team members refused to speak to him, fans in the stands laughed at him, called him names, hurled objects at him, threatened him, and threw black cats onto the field when he stepped up to bat. Robinson's response was to remain calm, and hit the ball harder. In 1947 he won the "Rookie of the Year" award and in 1949 he was voted the National League's "Most Valuable Player." Jackie Robinson's success opened the doors for other African Americans in major league sports.

Jackie Robinson was the first African American in a major league sport, General Benjamin O. Davis, Sr. was the first African American general in the U.S. Army, and President Barack Obama was the first

African American president. This does not mean they were the first African Americans with the ability to excel in their positions. Instead, they were the first African Americans who were allowed the opportunity to excel in their particular fields.

Jackie Robinson

Assigning children to schools based on the color of their skin is not in keeping with "all people are created equal" in The Declaration of Independence. Nonetheless, the U. S. Supreme Court upheld the idea of separate facilities in the case of Plessy v. Ferguson (1896). According to this decision, it was legal to have separate train cars for African Americans and European Americans so long as the train cars were of equal quality. This ruling in transportation was applied to all other public facilities.

African Americans disliked the 1896 **"separate but equal"** ruling because the whole idea of segregation is based on the lie that African Americans are not as good as European Americans.

The second distasteful thing about "separate but equal" is that schools established for Children of Color were never equal to other schools. Often the African American school was a church basement or a school that had been abandoned when a new school was built for children who were not of color. In most cases, schools for African American children had poor lighting, poor ventilation, poor heating, and old, outdated textbooks. Fewer tax dollars were spent per child on the education of African American children than on the education of European American children.

By 1950 lawyers from *The National Association for the Advancement of Colored People*, led by **Attorney Thurgood Marshall**, were attacking the principle of segregation itself. These attorneys argued that separate schools would always be unequal because segregation implies that one group of people is superior to another group of people. They made their argument before the U.S. Supreme Court on behalf of seven-year-old Linda Brown.

**Linda Brown** lived in Topeka, Kansas. She had to cross dangerous

Railroad tracks are extremely dangerous for children

railroad tracks and walk six blocks in order to catch a school bus that took her to a "Colored School" several miles from where she lived. Segregation required this even though a school designated for European Americans was within safe walking distance of her home.

The world waited as Supreme Court justices deliberated over the issue of segregation in American public life.

Catching the school bus to maintain segregation

On May 17, 1954, the United States Supreme Court handed down its ruling in *Brown v. Board of Education*. The nine white justices agreed that separating students in public schools on the basis of color was a violation of the U.S. Constitution. This decision set the standard for all public facilities in this country and led to a major change in American social life.

Many European Americans in the South responded to the *Brown v. Board of Education* ruling with anger and defiance. Governors and other state politicians made it clear that they would fight against desegregation. People of African descent who sought to enroll their children in "White" schools were fired from their jobs. Others were denied credit from banks and evicted from their homes. But this did not stop African Americans from enrolling their children. In the mid-1970s when the courts required children to be bused to different neighborhoods in order to desegregate schools, Boston, Massachusetts was a northern city that also responded violently to desegregation.

In 1957, a federal court judge ordered **Central High School** in **Little Rock, Arkansas** to admit nine African American students. Many European Americans in that city, armed with chains, guns, and homemade bombs, surrounded the school to prevent the nine teenagers from entering the building. This mob violence caused **President Dwight Eisenhower** to protect the African American students with federal troops.

In January of 1961, European Americans at the University of Georgia responded violently when two African American students, **Charlayne Hunter** and **Hamilton Holmes**, registered at that school. There was also a violent response at the University of Mississippi when **James Meredith** registered for classes in September of 1962. A few months later, the governor of Alabama personally blocked the door to the University of Alabama to prevent **Vivian Malone** and **James Hood** from enrolling. **President John F. Kennedy** sent federal troops to protect the African American students and to enforce the law.

Little Rock, Arkansas – 1957

# Precious Children,

My brown skin reminds me of courageous people who kept going when mobs were spitting on them, yelling hateful words toward them, hitting them, and threatening them. Linda Brown's family and the other plaintiffs in Brown v. Board of Education, the Little Rock Nine, Charlayne Hunter, Hamilton Holmes, James Meredith, Vivian Malone, and James Hood are amazing heroes. They make me proud of my brown skin.

The people I have told you about thus far were extraordinarily remarkable. They stood tall on their feet as they survived, succeeded, and contributed to society. The lady I want to tell you about now changed this nation by sitting rather than standing. She sparked an entire movement.

**Mrs. Rosa Parks** was a Montgomery, Alabama seamstress who rode to and from work every day on a city bus. On December 1, 1955, Mrs. Parks had no plans of changing her life or the life of her nation. After getting on the segregated bus to ride home, she found a seat at the front of the section where African Americans were allowed to sit. Moments later, when the driver picked up a European American male passenger, he told Mrs. Parks to get out of her seat and let the new man sit down. She refused. Mrs. Parks said she had paid the same fare as

Mrs. Rosa Parks

everyone else, she was in the seat first, and she would not move. Police officers were called and Mrs. Parks was arrested and taken to jail.

**Dr. Martin Luther King, Jr.** (a local Baptist preacher) and other city leaders rallied around Mrs. Parks. For an entire year, Dr. King led the people of Montgomery in a bus boycott. They walked to work, to church, and to shopping areas. They refused to ride city buses until all people could sit in any passenger seat on the bus. I am amazed at what they did. They walked in the rain, they walked in the hot sun, they walked when strong winds were blowing, and they walked when the weather was cold. They walked for more than 365 days. When the bus company started losing money, spokesmen for the company complained and said the people had no right to walk. I always thought that was funny. The people in Montgomery must have thought so, too, because they kept walking. What they did was truly incredible.

Television cameras recorded the bus boycott and it was shown on the evening news. People throughout the world began to question American democracy and call for fair play in this country. During this boycott, lawyers for The *National Association for the Advancement of Colored People* (NAACP) argued in the courts against segregated seating on buses.

In 1956, the Supreme Court ruled that local laws requiring segregation on buses were unconstitutional. Bus passengers of all colors could sit wherever they wanted to sit.

While many African Americans were concerned with integration, Malcolm X stressed the importance of black people establishing their own farms, bakeries, stores, restaurants, manufacturing plants, hospitals, and schools. He wanted African Americans to be independent of European American influence.

Malcolm X was a brilliant orator. He was insightful and he had an amazing way of conveying his thoughts in words his listeners would remember. What he said resonated with people who had been treated unjustly. He eventually let go of anger toward those who had wronged him in the past, and he saw all people as brothers and sisters without regard to skin color.

Malcolm X

• • •

# Precious Children,

I am grateful for Mrs. Parks and I am grateful for Dr. King. I am grateful for the people in Alabama who supported the Montgomery bus boycott. These people defeated segregation by refusing to ride. They just walked. I am also grateful to Malcolm X for his stirring, thought-provoking words.

My brown skin reminds me of all those times when people allowed their lights of love to shine in a world that was mean and hateful. When I was a child, my parents taught me to sing, "This little light of mine, I'm going to let it shine. Let it shine, let it shine, let it shine." I want you to remember these words, and always let your light shine for what is right. I like my brown skin: I like me.

Dr. Martin Luther King, Jr.

## CHAPTER 11

# I Like My Brown Skin Because...

## It Reminds Me Of The Bravery African Americans Showed During The Civil Rights Movement.

# I Am Also Brave.

**Dr. Martin Luther King, Jr.** practiced a philosophy of non-violent direct action. He and other civil rights leaders organized groups of people to break unfair laws in order to highlight existing injustices. The goal was to break the law in broad daylight, get arrested, and go to jail – all in front of television cameras. The intent was that when the larger society realized that people were suffering because of an unfair law, the law would be changed. So Dr. King encouraged sit-ins, kneel-ins, wade-ins, pray-ins, read-ins, etc. He led people to "White" amusement parks, "White" libraries, and any other institutions that were closed to People of Color. Dr. King was a **visionary** and a **strategist**. He dreamed great things for the future and he had a logical plan of action for making his dream come true. During the **Civil Rights Movement**, people of all colors marched with Dr. King to protest segregated facilities. Everywhere he spoke he encouraged people to get involved in the Civil Rights Movement. This movement would allow **all Americans to exercise their rights as citizens.**

Eating at **public lunch counters** is a legal right of all Americans. But when neatly dressed African American college students sat down to eat, waitresses refused to serve them. Some European American

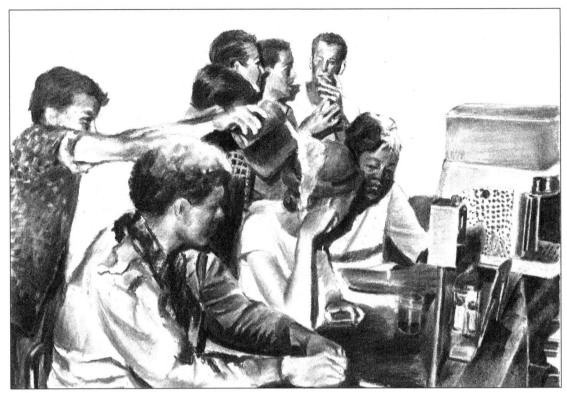

Eating at public lunch counters is a legal right, but when neatly dressed African American college students sat down to eat, waitresses refused to serve them.

customers spat on the students. Others poured mustard, ketchup, and soft drinks on their clothes and burned their skin with cigarettes. The demonstrators' lives were in danger.

But the students refused to leave. They were brave and they had a moral purpose. As soon as one group of sit-in demonstrators was arrested, another group took its place. In jail, **sit-in demonstrators** went on hunger strikes to call world attention to their goal of peacefully ending segregation. Cameras recorded what was happening and the demonstrations were shown on evening news programs. After watching the news, people throughout the world began asking how U.S. soldiers could fight for democracy abroad when African Americans were denied democracy at home. Eventually, court orders made it clear that

This bus was burned and the "Freedom riders" on board were beaten by an angry mob in Birmingham, Alabama.

businesses open to the public must serve everyone or close their doors. These court orders brought an end to segregated lunch counters.

To test the desegregation of interstate transportation, integrated groups of American college students became **"Freedom Riders."** They rode buses throughout the South and sat next to each other on the buses. Angry mobs met the **"Freedom Riders"** at the bus stations. They beat up the students and set the buses on fire. But this did not stop them. They kept riding throughout the South and they kept ignoring the signs for "Colored" and the signs for "White" that were posted on restroom doors at the stations. In September 1961, the Interstate Commerce Commission prohibited segregation in bus and train stations nationwide.

Civil Rights activists marched to bring attention to the fact that African Americans were denied their constitutional rights.

The one-hundredth anniversary of the Emancipation Proclamation was to be celebrated in 1963. During that year Congress was debating a civil rights bill that President John F. Kennedy had proposed.

A. Phillip Randolph, the man who had called for a massive march on Washington in 1941, was becoming impatient with Congress's delay in passing the civil rights bill. Most other Americans who believed in "…liberty and justice for all" were becoming impatient, too.

Randolph and civil rights leader **Bayard Rustin** called for a **March on Washington for Jobs and Freedom**. This March would demonstrate to Congress how much the civil rights bill was needed. Menial jobs were still assigned to People of Color, and upwardly mobile jobs were still reserved for European Americans. Banks denied loans to African Americans, and they did not have access to quality housing,

More than 250,000 people of all colors and ethnic backgrounds assembled in Washington, D.C. on August 28, 1963 for the historic *March*. Black people, brown people, white people, yellow people, red people, and every color in between came from every state in America and from several foreign countries.

Speakers from civil rights groups, religious organizations, and labor unions told the world of the injustices People of Color were suffering. Then they called for the passage of the civil rights bill before congress. One highlight of the March was the **"I Have a Dream"** Speech by Dr. Martin Luther King, Jr. In this speech, Dr. King called for all people in America to be judged by the "content of their character rather than by the color of their skin."

All people in the United States benefited from the *Civil Rights Movement* that was led and symbolized by Dr. King. This movement

Mrs. Fanie Lou Hamer

unlocked chains that restricted African Americans. It also unlocked many more chains that restricted European Americans. When African Americans began to exercise their rights as citizens, other groups of people who felt left out began to demand their rights, too. Groups that supported women's rights, the rights of the physically and mentally challenged, gay rights, senior citizen rights, children's rights, student rights, consumer rights, and workers' rights all increased their efforts as a result of the Civil Rights Movement.

By mid-summer 1964, the civil rights bill had passed both houses of Congress and was promptly signed by President Lyndon B. Johnson.

The purpose of the **1964 Civil Rights Act** was to protect all Americans from discrimination in employment and the use of public facilities. It outlawed discrimination in hotels, restaurants, amusement parks, theaters, skating rinks and most other businesses that served the public or received federal tax money. This included private companies that had contracts with the federal government.

The 1964 Civil Rights Act was followed by the **1965 Voter Rights Act.** This law was needed because some states made it difficult for African Americans to vote. They required them to pay a **poll tax** and/ or pass a **"literacy" test**. The "literacy" test often had questions no one would be expected to answer – like name the 88 counties in this state and the board of elections chairperson in each county. Or unanswerable questions like how blue is blue, how far is far, and how many bubbles are in a bar of soap.

When **Mrs. Fanie Lou Hamer**, an African American sharecropper, tried to vote in Mississippi, police officers beat her so badly that her kidneys were damaged. **Medgar Evers, James Cheney, Michael Schwerner**, and **Andrew Goodman** were killed in that state because they helped people register to vote.

On March 7, 1965, **John Lewis** began leading 600 marchers on a 54-mile walk from **Selma, Alabama** to Montgomery, Alabama. They were calling attention to the fact that African Americans in Selma were not allowed to vote. Alabama state troopers attacked these protesters on **"Bloody Sunday"** as they crossed the bridge to leave Selma. John Lewis was badly beaten on the head and in the face. Pictures of state

After the Voter Rights Act was signed into law, these young men were passionate about the importance of voting.

troopers beating innocent men, women, and children with their nightsticks flashed on television screens throughout the world. World opinion prompted the United States Congress to act. The **1965 Voter Rights Act** became law in August, and it removed all obstacles to voting. In 1987, John Lewis was elected to the U.S. Congress from Georgia, and in 2015 he was still supporting the agenda for civil rights in the nation's highest legislative body.

• • •

# Precious Children,

I will always be grateful for the brave people who participated in the Civil Rights Movement. They knew policemen would instruct vicious German shepherd dogs to attack them, and they knew firemen would hurt them with water from powerful fire hoses. They knew they would be arrested and thrown into jail. But they still participated.

I will always be grateful for the leadership of Dr. Martin Luther King, Jr., and all other leaders who supported him. I will always be grateful for freedom riders who tested desegregation even though they knew they would be beaten at the end of the bus ride. I will always be grateful for students who sat-in at lunch counters. I will always be grateful for young men and women of all colors who registered people to vote. I will always be grateful for the thousands of people I saw at the March on Washington in 1963. People with brown skin like mine were brave people who used their brains to overcome injustices. I like my brown skin: I like me.

Supreme Court Justice Thurgood Marshall, the brilliant lawyer who argued Brown v. Board of Education

## CHAPTER 12

# I Like My Brown Skin Because...

## It Reminds Me Of People Who Believe In Themselves Enough To Achieve Greatness.

# I Believe In Myself, Too.

As a result of the Civil Rights Movement, well-qualified African Americans became more visible in this country and their leadership roles increased.

In 1967, **President Lyndon Johnson** appointed the first African American justice to the Supreme Court. He was Thurgood Marshall, the brilliant lawyer who had argued Brown v. Board of Education before that court in the early 1950s.

From their earliest existence, American corporations refused to hire African Americans for administrative and managerial positions, even if they had federal government contracts. After the 1964 Civil Rights Act, such major American corporations as IBM, AT&T, Coca Cola, General Motors, The Chrysler Corporation, Georgia Pacific, Ford Motor Company, General Electric, Norfolk Southern, and Procter and Gamble ended their policy of ignoring People of Color. They began hiring highly qualified African Americans in professional positions. Other companies did the same thing: they interviewed outstanding

Ann Fudge enjoyed tremendous success at the helm of several major companies.

black students on college campuses and hired them. The People of Color they hired had brilliant minds and they increased the profits of the corporations that hired them.

**Jonathan A. Rogers** was president of CBS Television Stations.

**Delano E. Lewis** was president and Chief Executive Officer (CEO) of National Public Radio.

**Barry Rand** was chairman and CEO of Avis Rent a Car.

**Richard Parsons** was president of Time Warner, the $15 billion empire whose holdings included *Time Magazine, Sports Illustrated,* Home Box Office, and Warner Brothers.

**Kenneth C. Frazier** was chairman of the board and CEO of Merck and Company, a giant pharmaceutical business.

**Clarence Otis** was CEO of Darden Restaurants, which owns Red Lobster, Olive Garden, and Long Horn Steak House.

**Ann Fudge** was president of the Maxwell House Coffee Company, and president of Beverages Desserts and Post Division of Kraft General Foods. She was also chairman and CEO of Young and Rubicam Brands, a major advertising company.

**Kenneth Chenault** was CEO and Chief Operating Officer (COO) of American Express. He led that company to unprecedented growth.

**Ursula Burns** was CEO of Xerox. She was the first African American woman to head a Fortune 500 Company. She increased her company's revenues to twenty-two billion dollars in 2012.

**Donald Cordell Thompson** was CEO of The McDonald's Corporation (McDonald's hamburger chain). In 2012, Thompson increased his company's revenues to more than twenty-seven billion dollars.

Ursula Burns was the first African American woman to head a Fortune 500 Company. She is chairman and CEO of the Xerox Corporation.

African American technicians and middle managers in these corporations were excellent, also. **Dr. Mark Dean** was an engineer at IBM when he acquired three patents for IBM's personal computer. The personal computer is one of the most significant technological developments in history.

People of Color insisted on textbooks that included the contributions of African Americans. They insisted on seeing African Americans

Kenneth Chenault is chairman and CEO of the American Express Corporation.

in commercials and advertising. They also pressed for television programming that featured African Americans in positive roles. Television networks responded with such programs as *I Spy, Hogan's Heroes, Star Trek, Mission Impossible, Julia, The Mod Squad, Room 222,* and *The Cosby Show*.

***The Cosby Show*** was a situation comedy about a professional African American couple and their five children. It was the highest

Dr. Mark Dean played a critical role in the development of one of the most important technological developments of our era – the personal computer.

ranked family comedy show of the 1980s, and it topped the Nielsen ratings for five consecutive seasons. It also received the People's Choice Award for seven of its eight years.

In 1959, **Berry Gordy** borrowed eight hundred dollars from family members and opened his **Motown** studio in Detroit. No one knew the impact his music would have on Americans of all colors. The Supremes, The Temptations, The Four Tops, Smokey Robinson and the Miracles,

Miss Oprah Winfrey

Martha and the Vandellas, The Jackson Five, Stevie Wonder, and various other musicians wrote, played, and sang music that touched the souls of all Americans. People throughout this country were dancing to the music they created. Motown music provided a spiritual connection between African Americans and European Americans.

**Oprah Winfrey** was a leading television personality in the 1990s whose message of peace, understanding, inclusivity, and forgiveness helped Americans live up to their best qualities as human beings. Her daytime talk show won every award for excellence in its category, and she became the first African American billionaire. Her program gave people of all colors an opportunity to talk together and think together about subjects that touched the human experience. In the human experience, all people laugh and all people cry. Miss Winfrey helped all people to recognize their shared humanity.

Most African Americans in this country are ordinary citizens who spend their lives doing what is right and living with very little fanfare. They are known only to their family members, friends, neighbors, church members, and co-workers. That is also true of all other Americans, regardless of color. However, there are many African Americans who have been so outstanding that they stand out like shining lights. Eight of them are pictured in the closing pages of this book.

More people bought copies of **Michael Jackson**'s album, "Thriller," than any other album in the history of the world. He is considered one of the greatest entertainers of all times.

Michael Jackson

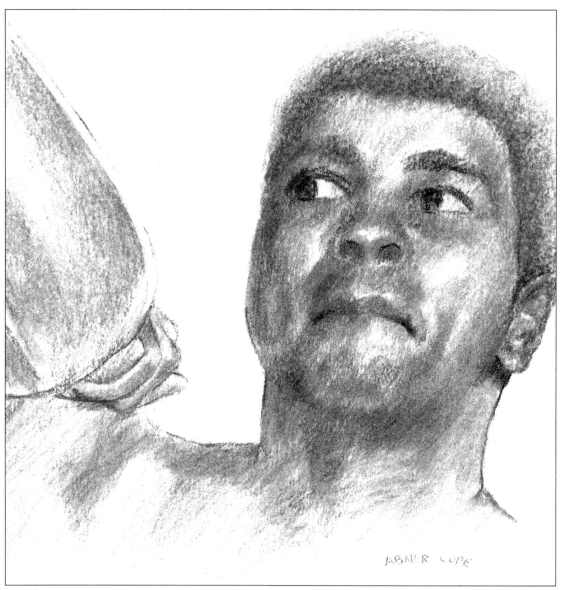

Muhammad Ali

**Muhammad Ali** was the only boxer in history to regain the world heavyweight championship title after it was taken away from him. It had been taken away because he opposed American military involvement in Vietnam. He stood up for his convictions, and today he is revered all over the world as one of the most outstanding human beings who ever lived.

Starting in 2014, **Serena Williams** won four Grand Slam tennis tournaments in a row: the U.S. Open, the Australian Open, the French Open, and the British Open (Wimbledon). So far, her career earnings total more than $73,000,000 (seventy-three million dollars) in prize money. Sports analysts say she is the greatest female tennis player of all times.

Serena Williams

In 1987, **Dr. Ben Carson** made medical history with an operation to separate a pair of Siamese twins who were joined at the back of the head. Operations to separate twins joined in this way had always failed, resulting in the death of one or both of the infants. Dr. Carson led a seventy-member surgical team that worked for twenty-two hours before the twins were successfully separated. Both of them lived.

Dr. Ben Carson

Dr. Mae Carol Jemison

**Dr. Mae Carol Jemison**, a physician, became the first African American woman to be admitted to the astronaut training program. On September 12, 1992, Miss Jemison flew into space with six other astronauts on an eight-day orbit aboard the spacecraft *Endeavour*. Dr. Jemison was the Science Mission Specialist on the flight. She was responsible for conducting weightlessness and motion sickness experiments on all *Endeavor* crewmembers.

Douglas Wilder

**Douglas Wilder** was elected governor of Virginia and served in that position from 1990-1994.

Deval Patrick was elected governor of Massachusetts in 2006 and he was elected for a second term in 2010.

As Chairman of the Joint Chiefs of Staff, **General Colin Powell** was the supreme military commander of the United States. He was appointed to this position by President George H.W. Bush. He was also Secretary of State for President George W. Bush.

General Colin Powell

Senator **Barack Obama**, an African American professor of constitutional law at the University of Chicago, was elected President of the United States in 2008 and elected again in 2012. While the majority of Americans of all colors voted for President Obama, his election and re-election did not mean there was an end to discrimination and prejudice in this country.

The first bill signed into law by **President Obama** was the Lily Ledbetter Fair Pay Act that made it difficult for employers to pay women less money than men for doing the same job. He insisted on the extension of health care with the Affordable Care Act (also called Obamacare) and the Health Care and Education Reconciliation Act. These two acts represented the most significant regulatory overhaul of the U.S. healthcare system since the passage of Medicare and Medicaid in 1965.

In addition, President Obama oversaw the bailout of the automobile industry. In response to a major recession and the bankruptcy or failure of three of the largest investment banks (Lehman Brothers, Bear Stearns and Merrill Lynch), President Obama's leadership led to the signing of the American Recovery Act and Reinvestment Act of 2009. The Obama Administration saw over 63 consecutive months of private sector job growth, a drop in the unemployment rate, a reduction of carbon pollution and the appointment of two women to the Supreme Court, including a woman of color.

● ● ●

President Barack Obama

# Precious Children,

I am proud of all the people whose names are in this book. They knew that skin color had nothing to do with letting their lights shine no matter where they were. You and I can do the same great things that others have done. We can be scientists, politicians, business leaders, spiritual leaders, educators, athletes, inventors, builders, organizers, social workers, psychologists, entertainers, financial geniuses, and anything else we want to be. We can be astronauts and fly to different planets. We can also do small things right where we live. Small things like loving every human being we see, small things like treating everybody right, and small things like wanting the best for all people regardless of their skin color. I like my brown skin: I like me.

# Epilogue

Precious children, my brown skin has helped me to be an amazing person. You are also amazing. The future is bright. Use your brain and your heart, be your best self, and enjoy your life!

In this book, you have read the awesome story of African Americans who survived and thrived against all odds. But in spite of victories already won, in the first half of the 21st century, there were still challenges for this nation.

● **Distrust existed between police officers and People of Color.** Since the beginning of the 21st century, hundreds of unarmed black men have been killed by police officers.

● The 2012 murder of **Treyvon Martin** made African Americans suspicious of "stand your ground" laws. One such law in Florida allowed a European American man to pursue and kill an unarmed African American teenager (Martin) who was carrying a bag of Skittles and a bottle of iced tea while talking on a cellular telephone.

● Due primarily to the advancements of computer technology and the outsourcing of labor, the United States has a **shortage of jobs**. People of all colors are unemployed. STEM training in science, technology, engineering, or math is most helpful for future employment.

● **"White privilege"** still exists in most American institutions. "White privilege" refers to the ways in which each aspect of this country was organized to benefit European Americans: banking; health care; housing; education; politics; commerce; agriculture; media services; religious institutions; medical services; disaster-relief services; the military; federal, state, and local government services; etc. On all levels, European Americans are still hired, trained, promoted, and assisted before African Americans. They are also given the benefit of the doubt when people are not sure what has happened. Time after time we see examples of European Americans committing crimes and blaming African Americans. Over the years, white officials have taken the word of the European American.

● There seems to be a **harsher standard of justice for People of Color than for white Americans**. African Americans have been imprisoned for acts that often don't even bring an indictment to European Americans. The difference in treatment is seen in the types of things people are arrested for, and the way they are arrested. This difference in treatment continues all the way through coming to trial, being convicted, receiving harsher sentences, and receiving less clemency from parole boards.

● **Some educators have low expectations for African American children** and do not encourage them to excel. **Some African American parents do not know how to be advocates for their children in the school system.**

Each one of these challenges is being addressed right now by community leaders, human relations organizations, civil rights leaders, religious leaders, educational leaders, social workers, grassroots organizations, political leaders, and people with signs marching in the streets for social justice. Americans have worked together to overcome challenges in the past, and Americans of all colors are still working together to overcome situations that are right here with us today. **Considering other negative situations Americans have conquered, I have no doubt that these current problems will also be solved.** The future will be even brighter than the present. **Do the work that is set before you, learn everything good that you can learn, be your best self at all times, use your brain and your heart, and enjoy your life!**

History is ever moving forward, and all of us choose the role we want to play in that history. The United States is at its best when we work together. In *I Like My Brown Skin Because…,* you have seen people of all colors work together to help the United States live out its ideals. **This book has given you excellent role models. What will you do with your life? What role will you play in loving yourself and all human beings on this earth?**

I love my brown skin. I love me, and I love you, too.

# Glossary of Words and Terms

**Arsenal.** A place where weapons are stored.

**Communion.** A religious sacrament in Christian churches.

**Croix de Guerre.** French military award for heroism in battle.

**Desegregation.** The elimination of laws, customs, or practices under which certain people are restricted to public facilities that are separate from the dominant society.

**Discrimination.** Making a distinction against a person based on the group, class, or category to which that person belongs rather than on individual merit.

**Emancipation.** The condition of being freed.

**Entrepreneur.** A person who organizes and operates a business.

**Financial literacy.** Knowledge in working with money; understanding buying and selling, saving and investing, interest rates, stocks, gains and losses, and what it takes to organize and maintain a business.

**Inherent.** Inborn, natural, intrinsic. When the West African father told his baby that no one on earth was inherently better than he was, he was saying that no one else was created with more talents than his child, and his child did not have to feel inferior to any other person.

**Militant.** Warring, physical fighting; violent.

**Non-Violent Direct Action.** This action was successfully used by Dr. Martin Luther King, Jr., Mahatma Gandhi, and Henry David Thoreau. Each one of these men intentionally broke unjust laws for all to see. Then they peacefully submitted to arrest and jail. They knew that when others saw them suffering because of an unfair law, pressure would be put on politicians to change that law. Dr. King used non-violent direct action in front of television cameras, and the laws were changed.

**Posthumously.** Occurring after the death of an individual.

**Produce.** Food from the land. Fruits, nuts, vegetables, and grains.

**Race.** Anthropologists and sociologists say there is only one race of people and that is the human race. All humans are alike under the skin. Their hearts, lungs, kidneys, and other vital organs can be interchanged. They can produce children together. All human beings have the same goals: life, liberty, and happiness.

**Segregation.** The act or practice of setting certain people apart from the main body or the main group.

**Smelt.** Extract metal from its ore by a process of heating and melting.

**Strategic.** Planned, calculated; an action that has smart planning behind it may be called "strategic."

**Visionary.** A person who has great ideas for the future; a person who looks at situations as they are and imagines ways that they can be changed for the better.

**Wholesale.** The selling of goods in quantity.

For bulk orders and shipping prices, please call (937) 215-3818 or visit www.epps-alford.com.

CPSIA information can be obtained
at www.ICGtesting.com
Printed in the USA
BVOW10*1036161116

467645BV00009BA/6/P